IKEBANA

IKEBANA

A New Illustrated Guide to Mastery

WAFU TESHIGAHARA

Photographs by Kaichi Ushiki

KODANSHA INTERNATIONAL
Tokyo and New York

Previously published as *Japanese Flower Arrangement*

Distributed in the United States by Kodansha International/USA, Ltd. through Harper & Row, Publishers, Inc., 10 East 53rd Street, New York, New York 10022.

This book was originally published in Japanese in 1965 by Kodansha under the title *Ikebana Dokushusho*. The present text has been translated and adapted for Western readers by Martin Cohen and the staff of Kodansha International, Tokyo. Copyright © 1966 by Kodansha Ltd. This English-language edition is published by Kodansha International Ltd., 2-2, Otowa 1-chome, Bunkyo-ku, Tokyo 112 and Kodansha International/USA Ltd., 10 East 53rd Street, New York, New York 10022. All rights reserved. Printed in Japan.

LCC 81-110645
ISBN 0-87011-438-7
Seventh printing, 1987   ISBN 4-7700-0915-1 (in Japan)

TABLE OF CONTENTS

JAPANESE IKEBANA

Japanese ikebana is a creative art which brings indoors the charm and beauty of landscapes, the seashore or lakeside. Ikebana recreates nature on a reduced scale through the arrangement of all types of plant material gathered from nature—from gardens, rivers, valleys. Nature is thus always close by for us to learn of its essence.

The young Japanese woman seen here arranging flowers gathered her ikebana material from the garden, as she does throughout the year. Most Japanese women study ikebana at one time or another, not so much for the beauty of the flowers but because arranging teaches them of the relationship between man and nature. Flower arrangements thus do more than decorate our homes—they provide moral sustenance as well.

HISTORY AND SPIRIT OF IKEBANA

NATURE, MAN AND FLOWERS

Is there anyone who does not think flowers beautiful? It would be strange if a person enjoyed animals and birds yet disliked flowers. Enjoying the beauty of flowers is common to all mankind.

Ikebana finds its basis in the beauty and meaning flowers have for man, a perceived beauty which stems from the essential bonds of man and nature. Nature is not only the wellspring of man's existence but also defines the vital spirit of beauty. Flowers, needless to say, represent such beauty.

THE ORIGIN OF IKEBANA

The primal beauty of nature as represented in flowers naturally results in the desire to have flowers near at hand. The act of cultivating, picking, or even buying flowers for any occasion is the act of making them our own, of putting them to a new use. The relation between flowers and our lives is thus developed and deepened.

But since flowers are living things, cut flowers or branches will quickly wither unless proper steps are taken to allow them to last as long as possible. The flowers, true to the meaning of the word *ike*bana, 'live' in the container.

This is a classic arrangement in a *tokonoma* decorated with a scroll.

THE EMERGENCE OF IKEBANA

Buddhism, introduced into ancient Japan from the Chinese mainland from the sixth and seventh centuries on, developed further in Japan, where it greatly influenced all aspects of life, culture and the arts.

Formal offertory flowers on the Buddhist altar combined with the aristocratic taste for floral decoration and fused into a refined form which evolved into ikebana.

In the thirteenth and fourteenth centuries, when Buddhism spread among the common people, the architectural style which became prominent was one which included the *toko-*

noma. In this 'alcove' Buddhist scrolls were hung and the custom arose of placing flowers there as offerings. In time the *tokonoma* took on a decorative function, the Buddhist scrolls were replaced by scroll paintings, calligraphy, and by antiques, and with this change the flowers placed in the *tokonoma* lost their religious meaning, leading to the development of flower arranging as an art.

The Development of Ikebana

Ikebana then developed with the *tokonoma* as its stage. At first a place where Buddhist scrolls were hung and offerings of flowers were made, the *tokonoma* gradually became a place for works of art—including ikebana—placed there to indicate respect for guests and their artistic sensitivity.

In this way, the room with the *tokonoma*, or the *tokonoma* itself, came to be considered the center of the house, and was respected as a symbol. At the heart of arranging flowers was the goal of presenting flowers appropriate to the season for the pleasure of guests. Ikebana thus developed with a sensitivity for the seasons and seasonal change, and for human relationships, at its core.

The cultural preferences of each age were manifested on the stage of the *tokonoma*, and the tradition of ikebana formed through the years has continued through the present. This tradition is to be seen in the varieties of arrangement styles and in the different kinds of containers which are used.

Flowers That You Like—Suitably— In a Container That You Like

The basic nature of ikebana as an expression of the seasons and as a social form soon resulted in its becoming restricted by various conventions. Today, however, ikebana contains a freer ability for self-expression.

While a bunch of miscellaneous flowers plopped haphazardly in some pot may be an expression of nature, the social and human requirements of ikebana at the same time demanded an esthetic. A flower arrangement had to be pleasing, and at best, transcendently pleasing.

From this has been derived the idea, 'arrange the flowers that you like—suitably—in a container that you like.' 'Flowers that you like' means you may arrange anything; your reasons may be that certain flowers are easy to obtain, or that you prefer certain flowers over others.

'Suitably' refers to quantity, as befits the place to be decorated and the container. An arrangement for a living room might contain many branches, but one for a writing desk might contain only one or two.

A 'container that you like' means that an expensive or a specially crafted container is not necessary. There are many miscellaneous articles which may be used as ikebana containers. Arrange flowers in whatever you like.

To sum up, you must enjoy the process of arranging and the result must be enjoyable to those around you. This, the 'flowers that you like—suitably—in a container that you like,' is the way of thinking of modern ikebana.

FLOWERS IN A JAPANESE MOOD

The names and adjectives used for flowers in Japan differ from those used in the West. Peony, by dint of its lushness and showiness, is called (literally), 'wealth and honor,' or 'the king of flowers.' Pine, because it is an evergreen and is a long-lived tree, is called 'tenacious,' or 'perennial youth.' These ideas came from China, and are expressions of Oriental thought.

The pine-and-peony combination is often used in painting, and in ikebana is a popular combination for the start of the year, when thoughts turn to spring. Moss covered pine and a single peony have been placed in a folkcraft straw container, originally a hat to protect its wearer from snow. This is a *moribana* arrangement.

Two Arrangements Using Magnolia

Magnolia branches have been used here in a classic compound arrangement—*moribana* for a round basin and *nage-ire* for the tall four-sided container.

Compound arrangements generally call for 2 groups in a single container, or *moribana* (or *nage-ire*) arrangements in 2 or more containers, but this is an exception. Different containers (but of the same color and material) and different types of ikebana (but with the same kind of material) have been used, resulting in excellent harmony. The special arrangement of the two is complementary, a key point in compound arrangements.

The Right Flowers for the Containers

The same material—bamboo—has been used for both containers, but one is delicate and one is straightforward in feeling. To match the charm of each, cornflowers and fresh cedrela foliage have been used in a compound *nage-ire* arrangement. The young foliage matches the delicate container, and the simplicity of the cedrela is appropriate to the bold container consisting of a single piece of bamboo. Selecting flowers which correctly match the container is an important aspect of arranging, and here it has been done particularly well.

Two Roses

Bamboo containers (like the two-level bamboo container pictured on page 23), have long been popular as traditional Japanese ikebana containers. This container's simple appearance is complemented by crescent-shaped decorations. To exactly match the 2 decorations, 2 roses have been used in this *nage-ire* arrangement. Some arrangers may think that 2 roses alone are insufficient, but once they are arranged in the container, it becomes evident that they are just enough and that no addition is needed.

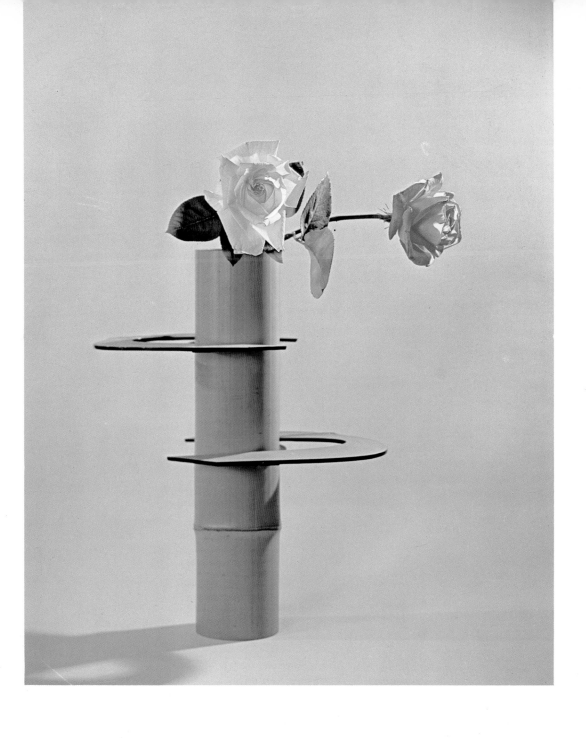

ARRANGING WATERSIDE SCENES

Japanese ikebana is considered to have the changing seasons as its base. In spring, spring flowers; in summer, summer flowers, obtained and used at the peak of their beauty—therein lies the way to experience the natural spirit of the flowers.

When summer comes, plants like the iris and blue flag which grow and bloom next to water burst forth in vivid life. This compound arrangement makes use of a classic type of container, made of the weathered wood of a boat, and two kinds of plants to recreate a waterside scene. By bending one of the bulrush stems, the impression of a breeze is imparted, especially fitting for a refreshing summer arrangement.

20

A Two-Level Arrangement

The idea of cutting a bamboo container so that arrangements could be placed at 2 points was thought of very soon after the establishment of ikebana art. Since then it has been widely used as a traditional container and can be considered to have created a prototype of the compound arrangement. Very Japanese-like flowers were used in this arrangement: lilies and daisies, plus maple leaves. Maple leaves are used in both parts, providing balance and continuity.

AUTUMN IN JAPAN

There may be nothing as replete with profound meaning as the idea that nature is a changing stage. The drama of change—from germination to the first buds, new leaves to autumn-tinged leaves—and the flow of life's strange forces develop before us in a beautiful way. It can be said that nature, for better or worse, is always changing.

Autumn in Japan, especially, is full of change. Fruit, foliage and flowers of the season are to be seen; autumn in Japan is truly a symphony of nature. This arrangement represents the variety found in autumn in its combination of the fruit and foliage of a grapevine and chrysanthemum flowers.

CAMELLIA AND NARCISSUS IN A BASKET
A lively and pleasant arrangement has been made
using an unusual variety of double-flowered camellia,
narcissus and ilex. To balance the volume of the
camellias, the narcissus have been arranged so as to be
fairly tall. The ilex acts as a link between the other
2 materials. Although this is a spreading arrangement and includes large and small flowers and berries,
it is actually relatively narrow and can be used in many
situations.

CHAPTER 1

WHAT IS A FINISHED ARRANGEMENT?

THE NATURE OF THE FLOWERS: THE BASIS OF THE ARRANGEMENT

Each plant and flower used in ikebana has its own distinctive beauty. There can be no ikebana if a flower's characteristic beauty is overlooked.

For example, when plants which bloom on the surface of water, such as water lilies, are used in ikebana, no one would think of putting them up on a shelf. The appearance of the lilies and water together is highly esteemed, and therefore a low basin-like container is used so that the flowers can be appreciated by viewing them from above.

When flowers are arranged, if consideration and respect is given to their natural state, their beauty is enhanced all the more. Whether it be sweet flag, azalea, cosmos, or bamboo, this is the meaning of capturing the plants' characteristic beauty.

We can devise any number of classifications for the endless variety and uncounted numbers of forms of plants, such as those which grow erect, those which grow along the ground, those with pendant flowers, etc. To fully utilize the special qualities of flowers, we can classify those with common qualities. After they are arranged and consideration is

31

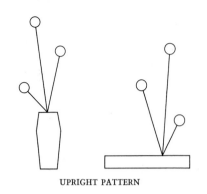

UPRIGHT PATTERN

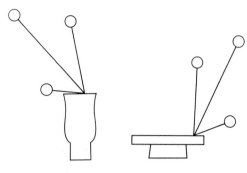

SLANTING PATTERN

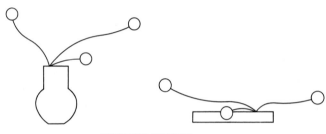

SPREADING PATTERN

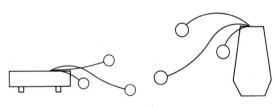

CASCADING PATTERN

HORIZONTAL PATTERN

given to a matching container, and the style determined, the result can be a work of art.

Irises or tulips, for example, are used in upright arrangements, spirea and willow in cascading arrangements and plants such as water lilies and candock are used in horizontal arrangements

Groups of plants with common characteristics determine the 5 basic patterns of finished arrangements:

upright pattern
slanting pattern
spreading pattern
cascading pattern
horizontal pattern

32

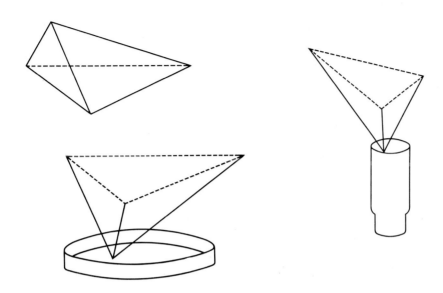

No matter who the arranger is or what the materials are, the result is one of these 5 patterns.

THE FRAMEWORK IS THREE STEMS
While utilizing and enhancing the nature of the flowers, there must be a framework for the composition by which they are combined to make a flower arrangement. This framework consists of 3 main stems. The plant materials used in ikebana—whether woody or herbaceous, branch or stem, with leaves or flowers—have an overall linear quality. The 3 main stems are used so as to take advantage of their linear qualities.

These 3 main stems—one long, one short and one intermediate in length—have their own characteristics, and by using these 3 as the framework of an arrangement, we can give the arrangement its outstanding unity.

Why is it that 3 stems are specified? In this connection, you must understand something of the general idea of three-dimensional form, because, in an exceedingly simplified sense, arranging flowers is nothing more than the creation of three-dimensional forms using plant materials.

DESIGNING WITH A 'PYRAMID'
Three-dimensional forms are shapes into

33

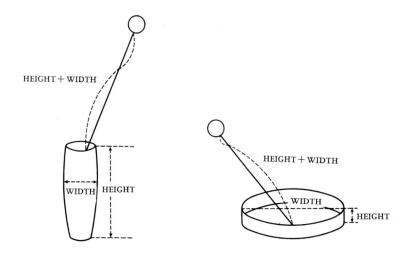

HEIGHT + WIDTH

WIDTH | HEIGHT

HEIGHT + WIDTH

WIDTH

HEIGHT

which you can put things. You cannot put any solid thing into a line, a point, or a surface, but three-dimensional forms permit you to place something within them for the purpose of display.

The simplest form of a standing arrangement is the inverted pyramid, a pyramid standing on its point. Other than the circle, there can be nothing simpler.

A pyramid is generally thought to have equal sides, but the pyramid to be used in ikebana is an oblique one, one with dissimilar sides which may have lengths such as 12, 6 and 3 inches.

Let us try making a pyramid above the container to be used. I am sure you can already visualize the arrangements that can be made. The 3 sides of the pyramid correspond, needless to say, to the 3 main framework stems of the arrangement.

As to why no more than 3 branches or stems are needed to create the framework, first of all, 3 is the minimum number needed to define a three-dimensional space, and also because, with 3 stems, just enough expressive strength is given to the plant material. There is no need to use 4 or 5 stems.

The 3 stems, the minimum needed, together form the body—the basic elements—of the finished arrangement.

How to Determine the Dimensions of the Arrangement

The long, medium and short stems should have the proportional lengths of 3—2—1, but when you make the arrangements, the actual lengths should be determined by considering the container selected.

First of all, the length of the longest stem should equal the width plus the height of the container. The length of the other 2 main stems can be easily determined by following the 3—2—1 formula. You should use this proportion for all containers, whether they are low and wide or tall and thin.

The 3—2—1 relationship has been determined to be the most esthetically pleasing proportion for ikebana, and by utilizing it, you can insure that arrangements will be attractive.

This proportion is for the lengths of the materials which extend outside the container when arranged. When cutting material, be sure to allow extra length for the portions which will be out of sight.

There will be exceptions, times when you will want to use as your long stem one which is 1½ times as long as the width plus the height of the container. In such a case you should carefully revise the lengths of the other 2 main stems so as to preserve the 3—2—1 proportion. Plants which can be used at such times include the chrysanthemum, carnation, dahlia and Chinese bellflower.

Needless to say, there are also times when changes must be made according to the nature of the materials used. For example, when using large flowers with intense colors, such as peonies, lilies and hydrangeas, or plants with large or many leaves, such as fatsia, or those with very thick stems, if they are not made somewhat shorter than the standard length, the arrangement's balance will be lost.

On the other hand, when you use fine-textured, pale-colored plants, such as bulrush, pampas grass, burnet, and patrinia, if they are not made a little longer, they will be overwhelmed by the container and again the arrangement's balance will be destroyed.

Such judgments are left to the artistic sense of the arranger. It is when the exceptions to the rules are correctly sensed and skillfully conceived and carried out that the pleasure of arranging flowers is truly felt.

THE BODY OF THE ARRANGEMENT

In actually making an arrangement, what are the essentials in working with the main stems?

In the first place, a flat arrangement, similar to an open fan, should not be made. Such flat arrangements give a feeling of weakness and instability, as if they would topple over at a touch. Similarly, a purely vertical arrangement is not pleasing because it gives the sense of being about to fall on its side.

By adjusting the main stems (after firmly fixing them at the base into the flower frog), fix them so as to form an inverted pyramid. Being careful to leave a space between them about as big as your fist, move the stems into whatever pyramid shape you like.

You will find that if you move your fist as far down between the stems as possible, the arrangement will acquire an open form, and if you move your fist as far up as possible, it will acquire a narrow form.

You should not worry about what materials to use for the 3 main stems. One, 2 or 3 varieties may be used. Thus, you may decide to use 3 dahlias, or a chrysanthemum, a Chinese bellflower and a pink. However, flower arrangements always have a central motif, and the materials must be selected according to this intended motif.

THE BODY'S 'ASSISTANT' AND THE FINISHED ARRANGEMENT

You have now learned about the functions and dimensions of the 3 main stems. But this isn't enough to make a flower arrangement. You have to add some flesh and blood to the skeleton. This is like the seasoning added to food, the supporting role played in the theater, or the accompanist at a recital. We call that which helps the body become even more beautiful the 'harmonizing helper' or 'assistant.'

This 'assistant,' unlike the body of the arrangement, is free from restrictions as to the length, number, variety or position of stems. You have the freedom to add flowers to the 'assistant' in any way you like when there is insufficient color or too much space between the stems of the body, or simply when you wish to use a favorite flower.

There is no limit to what may be done with the 'assistant' as long as the result is the beautification of the arrangement's framework. Providing that the balance and harmony between the arrangement's body and complementary elements are not lost, even an 'assistant' stem longer than the longest main stem may be inserted.

Ikebana consists of the body (the 3 main stems) and the 'assistant.' The 3 stems are used to make an oblique pyramid within which a finished arrangement is created and displayed, and the 'assistant' provides a harmonious complement to the body.

Ikebana Composition
Body (main stems)....long stem
                      medium stem
                      short stem
'Assistant' ....No restrictions on variety, number, length or arrangement of plant material.

DIFFERENCES BETWEEN THE FIVE FINISHED PATTERNS

Now that you understand that ikebana consists of the 3 main stems of the body and the 'assistant,' let's take up the 5 patterns of finished arrangements a little more exactly. Since the main purpose of ikebana is the best utilization and display of the qualities of plants, the treatment of the body and 'assistant' as well must have as its basis the aim and spirit of exploiting the plants' characteristic beauty. The finished arrangement, as has been mentioned, invariably falls into one of the 5 basic patterns: upright, slanting, spreading, cascading or horizontal.

However, how do you determine what pattern to use for your arrangement? The basis of deciding is the angle made by the long stem of the body with an imaginary vertical line drawn to the base of the branch. It is the position of the long stem which determines if the pattern is upright, slanting, cascading, or spreading. Horizontal arrangements are an exception to this rule.

Let's differentiate the 5 patterns on this basis.

In upright arrangements, the body is erect, and the angle between the imaginary vertical

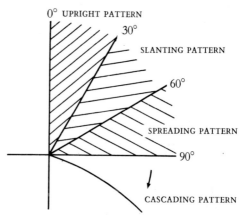

ARRANGEMENT PATTERNS AS DETERMINED BY THE POSITION
OF THE LONG STEM

line and the long stem should not exceed 30 degrees. The medium and short stems can be arranged at an even greater angle from the vertical, but the arrangement is still considered to be a standing one. Irises are typical of the plants used for this pattern.

Slanting arrangements are those in which the long stem is 30 to 60 degrees from the imaginary vertical line, no matter how the rest of the body is arranged—even if the other main stems are arranged vertically.

The stems of spreading arrangements extend to the sides of the container, and may be arranged from a horizontal position to one 60 degrees from the vertical, to make a shallow pattern.

The long stem of a cascading arrangement must extend below the horizontal. Arrangements in wall-hanging or suspended containers are usually of this pattern.

In horizontal arrangements the finished arrangement is spread over the surface of the water in the container. This arrangement is thus not determined by the angle the long stem makes with the vertical.

37

EXAMPLE OF AN UPRIGHT ARRANGEMENT
These irises arranged in a dragon-basket form a *mori-bana* arrangement. Irises are often used in upright arrangements, which enables one to utilize the characteristic lines of the leaves and stems of this type of plant. Iris can be used in *moribana* or *nage-ire* ikebana.

EXAMPLE OF A SLANTING ARRANGEMENT

The slanting arrangement is one which we see very often. The main stems enclose a space somewhat broader than in an upright arrangement. Here, a container with legs was used; the flower is amaryllis. The long amaryllis represents the long stem, the leaf seen on the left, the medium stem, and the shortest flower (to the front), the short stem of the body. This is a *moribana* arrangement, but amaryllis may also be used for *nage-ire* arrangements.

EXAMPLE OF A SPREADING ARRANGEMENT

Lilac has been used in this spreading arrangement, in the *nage-ire* style, which utilizes an ornamental vase. By using a spreading arrangement for the lilac, heavy with flower clusters, the flowers' beauty is further enhanced. Also, pine, azalea, climbing rose, hydrangea and other flowers which grow in a spreading fashion, as well as allium, sweet sultan and carnation, are good to use in this type of ikebana. These materials may also be used in *moribana* arrangements.

EXAMPLE OF A CASCADING *NAGE-IRE* ARRANGEMENT

Pine and rose have been used in this cascading *nage-ire* arrangement. The idea for this placement of the pine branch came from the way many pine trees in Japan are trained to gracefully spread their branches over adjacent lakes, ponds or canals. Roses provide a fresh counterpoint to the pine, here well used in accordance with its individual character.

EXAMPLE OF A HORIZONTAL ARRANGEMENT

This horizontal arrangement in the *moribana* style uses only water lilies and *sasa* bamboo in a white container. Water lilies, lotus and similar water plants which bloom in the summer are usually used in horizontal arrangements. Accordingly, horizontal arrangements are considered appropriate for the summer months. Horizontal arrangements are made only in the *moribana* style, never in the *nage-ire* style.

SIMPLIFIED ARRANGEMENTS

Though flowers are generally arranged according to the stated limits of a 3-stem framework and within one of the 5 finished patterns, the great variety of flower types, the requirements imposed by the container used, and the nature of the place where the arrangement is displayed sometimes demand a breaking of the standard rules.

When an arrangement's body is well made and the 'assistant' complements it, the arrangement is referred to as a standard arrangement. When something has been deliberately omitted from the body, the arrangement is called 'abbreviated,' and when only leaves or flowers are used for the body, the arrangement is called 'adapted.'

As a rule, the complete arrangement consists of the body and appropriate 'assistant,' but it is permissible to make an arrangement consisting of body alone. Following this line of thinking, it is possible to omit one of the main stems of the body to make an arrangement with only 2 main stems, or to omit 2 stems and arrange just one flower in the container.

Further, when using just one or two flowers, often the attached leaves or branches of the materials used are made to function in place of the omitted elements.

We can often see an adapted arrangement where the branches or stalks of the body have been replaced by a leaf or leaves, or by a flower corolla. Even if branches, stalks, leaves or flowers alone are used, the basic rule that ikebana is composed of 3 elements—the

Example of an arrangement where one of the main stems has been omitted. A purple and a white clematis have been used in a cascading *nage-ire* arrangement.

body, 'assistant' and container—does not change.

Ikebana consisting of only one branch and one flower can be considered a combination of the abbreviated and adapted arrangements.

CHAPTER 2

TOOLS AND TECHNIQUES

CONCERNING THE TOOLS

Let us look at the tools needed for ikebana, starting with the essential ones, the scissors and frogs.

There are 2 types of special ikebana scissors, as shown in the photo. They can be easily used to cut both thick branches and delicate stems.

However, the scissors with the large crescent-shaped handles are not recommended as they limit the movement of the hand, and when some trimming of a finished arrangement must be done, the handles get in the way.

You should have both sun-and-moon and rectangular frogs.

The sun-and-moon frog is a combination of a round and a crescent-shaped frog, both of which can be used individually in small containers. The rectangular frog is for wide containers and can also be used in compotes.

When you have scissors and frogs, you are ready to start arranging.

CONTAINERS: BASINS, VASES, COMPOTES

Generally, the most practical container for *moribana* arrangements is a wide, round basin, and for *nage-ire* arrangements, a cylindrical vase. There is also the versatile compote used for *moribana* arrangements.

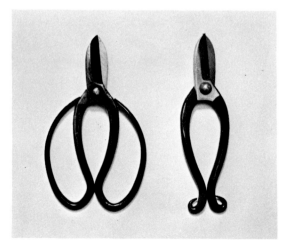

47

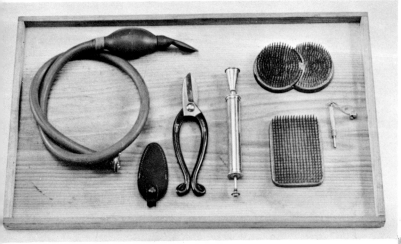

OTHER ESSENTIALS

In addition, a water pump, pin-straightener for the frog, and a water syringe are needed. A protective case for the scissors is also recommended.

Since you will be working with water, don't forget a plastic tablecloth or cover. (A tray on which to lay out the flowers beforehand is often useful as well.) Some arrangements call for the use of sand or pebbles in the container; aquarium sand can be used in such instances.

THE BEST WAY TO USE THE SCISSORS

Let's practice the use of the scissors. It is not as simple as it may seem.

1. Grasp one handle between the base of both thumb and forefinger, firmly enough so the scissors don't fall.

2. Your fingertips should rest on the other handle with just a little pressure; they are to move it when you want to cut.

3, 4. With your fingers, draw the lower handle closer to you until the scissors are closed.

That is all there is to it, but you must move the handles lightly. If you try to chop strongly, these scissors will be hard to use. Although some people may be seen using the scissors with their forefinger between the handles, this is not good because it reduces the power you can apply and makes cutting difficult.

CUTTING TECHNIQUES

Herbaceous material is cut straight across, at right angles to the stem (1). Cutting at an oblique angle is better for preservation of flowers, but does not permit the material to be firmly held by the frog. Thus, even soft material can be firmly held in place.

Except for very thin stems and branches, cutting is done at the base of the blades, with one motion. The feel when cutting this way is better and the pressure and weight of the scissors is fully utilized. In the case of slender material, pressure is not important and cutting can be done easily at the tips of the blades.

Slanting cuts for material as thick as a pencil
Stems and stalks about as thick as a pencil, a size often used in ikebana, are not cut straight across (2). Cut at the base of the scissor blades and in one motion, always at a 45 degree angle. Because the wood fibers are strongest —most resistant to cutting—at right angles to the branch, more effort is needed to cut straight across rather than at the 45 degree angle recommended here, and the scissors are dulled quickly. Further, if cutting is done

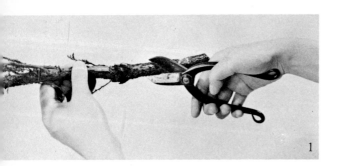

at the scissors' tip, much more strength must be exerted and the pressure of the scissors cannot be utilized.

Stems which cannot be cut with one stroke

Sometimes a stem thicker than a pencil cannot be cut with one stroke, even by cutting obliquely. In such a case, holding the stem firmly, make a cut, carefully remove the stem from the scissors (p. 49, [3]), replace it firmly at the base of the scissors and cut again (p. 49, [4]). If yet another cut is needed, repeat this procedure. After you have cut 2 or 3 stems

you will be able to cut properly and without difficulty.

Cutting very thick stems

Some stems and branches are too thick even for the above method to be used. Branches as thick as one or two fingers are usually cut with a saw, but by the following method you can easily cut them with scissors. Let us practice with an evergreen branch.

1. Position the scissors where you want to cut and make a small cut to mark the place.

2. Hold the branch firmly with the other

50

1. Trim twigs at the base.
2. Be sure that no trace of cutting shows on branches.

3. Remove leaves in the same way, at their base.
4. Don't leave any leafstalks on the material.

hand, and so that the foliage will be down, out of the way. Keep elbows close to your body. Shift the position of the hand holding the scissors so that the back of the hand is opposite the branch and almost touching it. Cut deeply enough to scar the branch.

3. Move the scissors to the opposite side and cut, putting some strength into it. Don't think you are going to cut through at once.

4. Cut deeply enough so that the scissors will remain in place even if your hand is taken away.

5. Since more than one cut is needed, take the scissors from the branch.

6. Insert the scissors in the same place and cut again, rotating the scissors in place from left to right as you cut. Repeat procedures 5 and 6 until the cut is completed.

The knack of holding the branch upside down and cutting from the bottom up, turn-

5, 6. Since herbaceous material is soft and tends to wilt easily, carefully trim such material according to the above rules.

ing the scissors from left to right, is a method of taking advantage of the weak points of the wood fibers. Without getting tired or dulling your scissors, even fairly thick branches can be cut this way.

TRIMMING BRANCHES AND LEAVES

Trimming branches and leaves is one of the important techniques of ikebana (Figs., p. 51).

Branches and herbaceous material are rarely used in the state in which they are obtained. Extra twigs and leaves, and injured leaves and branches, must be completely removed before arranging can begin.

The result of not preparing materials beforehand is often just a confused jumble of flowers. Since the desired result is a beautiful arrangement of very specific materials,

it is advisable, to freely adjust and shape each branch or stem to be used. Especially, the lower leaves should be trimmed.

The removal of excess branches and leaves also helps in conserving the water contained within the plant.

Trim branches and leaves where they are joined to the main branch or stem. Stubs of branches and leaf stalks are unsightly. If the scar at a cut end of a branch is quite obvious, it should be covered with black ink.

BENDING BRANCHES

Because the principle of ikebana is to utilize and enhance the natural beauty of plants, it is unpleasant if the materials are twisted into unnatural shapes. However, there are times when it is necessary to bend branches.

When a little bending will make a branch more beautiful, or make it fit the container better, bending may be done. This is not to say that one should make the mistake of bending a straight branch into a curved shape, but an already curving branch may be enhanced by making it curve a little more. The method used varies according to the thickness of the branch.

Bend small branches in your palm (Figs., p. 52)
When you want to bend a narrow branch as in (1) a little more, hold it as in (2) and gently bend it. It is essential that both your palm and the branch be very wet. Bend the branch with short, quick motions.

Do this 4 or 5 times, evenly and at different places slightly above and below the starting point, until the branch has the curve you want (3).

Twist pencil-thick branches while bending them
Branches about as thick as a pencil should be grasped with thumbs just touching, and with your arms close to your body. Bend and twist the branch at the same time. Twisting breaks down the wood fibers while the bending is done. In this case also, both the branch and your palm should be wet.

1. This is a yew branch, about as thick as a pencil.

2. Holding it near the body, the thumb indicates the spot where the branch will be bent. The other hand grasps the branch in the same way.

3. Exerting a little strength at the finger-tips, the branch is slowly bent and twisted at the same time.

4. When you feel that the wood fibers

have been somewhat weakened, move your hands an inch or so and repeat the process. It is more efficient if your right hand is kept just about touching your stomach. Don't be concerned if the bark occasionally splits a little. The part which has been twisted won't break.

5. The branch has been bent to the desired curve. If you bend the branch suddenly, with thumbs apart, it will break. Take your time and bend gently and there will be no trouble in bending branches of this thickness.

Bending thick branches over a table edge
When thick branches are to be placed in ikebana containers, they sometimes must be bent. Being thick, they cannot be bent by twisting, so the following method is used.

1. This is the thick holly branch which is to be used.

2. Plan the most attractive arrangement of the branch in the vase. This holly branch lends itself to the kind of arrangement pictured.

3. Insert the branch in the vase, and determine the places, direction, and degree it is to be bent.

4. With the scissors, cut about $\frac{1}{3}$ through the branch, where it is to be bent, applying the scissors 2 or 3 times as needed.

5. Holding it at the edge of a table or box, bend it with quick, small motions. A cloth on the table will keep your hand from slipping.

6. Next, about an inch or an inch and a half away, repeat the above 2 steps.

7. It is now bent at 2 places.

8. Placed in the vase, the branch is in the desired position. Since the cut places are within the vase, no one will see them. In this way, ikebana cleverly conceals unnatural things.

9. If you think a branch has not been bent enough, insert a small wedge in the cut to

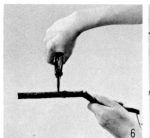

give it the desired form. If a branch much larger than this is to be used, make the cut with a saw so that the branch can be easily bent by hand.

Ways to Preserve the Water in Cut Plant Materials

Ikebana has value so long as it is living. Nothing is as unpleasant as a drooping or lifeless flower. In order to make living and vivid arrangements there are several very important things to do to the material before arranging.

Once cut, plants live for only a short time, even if supplied with water. Because ikebana uses cut plants, it employs techniques to take the most effective advantage of the plants' water supply. The methods of conserving water have been devised according to the respective plants' different propensities to hold water. However, there is one method of water conservation used for all plants—

cutting under water—which must be per-
formed before any other method. Cutting
under water is the most basic, and the most
effective, method of conserving the water in
plant materials.

Cutting under water
Cutting the base of flower stems, branches or
stalks under water ensures that water, not air
that obstructs the conservation of water,
will be taken up into the stem.

If plants are cut in the air, no matter how
quickly the cut stems are inserted in water,
air will have already entered the stem.
This air becomes a hindrance, and flowers
with a weak ability to take up water will not
be adequately supplied. The deeper the
material is in water, the better. The water
pressure augments the plant's ability to absorb.

When working with purchased or picked
materials, always cut the stems under water
before arranging. After this step, there are

other procedures devised to match the differing requirements of plants.

Applying salt
This is a simple method of conserving water,
effective with summer flowers such as dahlias.
Apply salt to the cut surface of the stem; the
result will be an increase in the plant's ability
to absorb water.

Singeing stems
Plants with relatively hard stems such as
peonies, should be singed with a flame.
Being careful not to burn the flowers, after
having wrapped the rest of the plant in a
towel or cloth, burn the bottom inch or two
of the stem until it is black. The trick is to
put the stem into water right after singeing it.

This is a method of shocking the plant
cells. Singeing not only disinfects the stem
but also allows the warmed air in the stem
to pass out of the plant relatively quickly, in-
creasing the plant's capacity to take in water.

Boiling stems

Many plants can be prepared at one time using boiling water. Insert the stems of the plants in about 1½ inches boiling water and wait 2 or 3 minutes, until the stems turn white. As when singeing stems, take care that the tops are not heated by wrapping them in a towel or other protective material. After the stems turn white, place the material in water.

Applying chemicals

There is also a means of fostering water conservation by applying compounds such as alcohol, table vinegar and peppermint oil. As in the case of salt, the ability of these compounds to disinfect and stimulate the absorption of water is utilized.

Alcohol is applied to ordinary materials. After cutting the stems in water, wipe all water from the base and apply alcohol for 2 or 3 seconds.

Wild flowers, such as thistles, are put in vinegar or acetic acid for a minute or two.

Peppermint oil is effective when applied to roses. Here also, apply it for only 2 or 3 seconds after thoroughly drying the bases of the stems. It can also be used for plants with weak stems, like calla lilies.

Water conservation for water lilies (Figs., p. 58)

Plants which grow in water, such as the water lily, have air-filled stems. There is a special method of water conservation, using this characteristic, which keeps the flowers looking fresh for a long time.

1. First, place the tobacco of 2 cigarettes on a cloth.

2. Wrap the tobacco in the cloth and immerse the cloth in water. Wring the cloth out over a coffee cup. Repeat several times until the cup is half-full.

3. Take the solution up in the syringe.

4. Inject the solution into the stem.

The solution will pass into the leaves in an instant.

The stem will fill like a sponge, and the nicotine solution will stimulate the plant cells and keep them alive for a long time. It will penetrate up to the base of the flower.

Water conservation for thick bamboo (Figs., p. 59) Bamboo is one of the worst plants regarding water conservation, so a special method is used. For bamboo from 2 to 4 inches in diameter, use the following method.

1. As the bamboo has many leaves, trim them as desired. The fewer the leaves, the easier it is to conserve water.

2. With a rod or pole, pierce all the nodes except the lowermost one.

3. Fill the bamboo to the top with salt water made by using one teaspoon of salt per cup.

4. Tamp a wad of cloth into the top as a stopper.

Add more salt water if needed later and the bamboo will stay fresh a long time. Be sure that the cloth doesn't show.

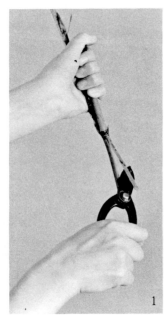

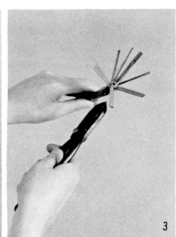

Water conservation for narrow bamboo

If you intend to collect the bamboo yourself, it should be done in the early morning or late in the day, after sunset. The bamboo should be cut under water and placed in deep water at once.

1. Immediately cut the lower 2 inches of the bamboo longitudinally. Cut each division thus made in half, and half again.

2. As if sharpening a pencil, cut away the pulp.

3. Next, spread the narrow pieces of the bamboo's hard exterior like the petals of a flower.

4. Place the bamboo in a can of water until you are ready to arrange it. The deeper the water, the better for water conservation.

60

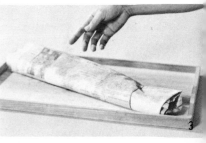

Restoring and Revitalizing Flowers

What is best for plants which have begun to wither before or after they have been arranged? Withered flowers do not take up water, so they must be revived before they can be arranged. This is the procedure:

1. First, hold the withered flowers upside down over a bowl or pail. Liberally pour water over the material.

2. Loosely wrap them in newspaper so that both flowers and stems are completely covered.

3. Pour water on the paper until it is soaking wet. Place the wrapped flowers on the floor in a damp or humid place, such as a bathroom. Do not place them in a draft or in the dark.

Having done this, water will enter even through the leaves and stems, and in most cases, the flowers will be fully freshened after 40 or 50 minutes.

Changing the Water

In order to keep arranged flowers for a long period, the water in the container must be completely changed daily. When a vase or compote is used and when the arrangements are hanging or suspended, use the pump (see illustration, p. 62).

Seven Rules for Making Excellent Arrangements

Even people whose course of study of ikebana was identical will attain greatly differing results. On the basis of my long experience in teaching ikebana I have summarized the way

61

to make excellent arrangements in 7 rules, presented below.

1. First, become experienced in using the scissors.

It is a commonplace thing, but being able to use the scissors freely is a shortcut to good arranging. And the saying 'Experience is the best teacher' holds true in this case. Eventually, whenever you pick up the ikebana scissors you should automatically use them in the proper fashion.

2. Branches and leaves should be trimmed without hesitation.

Ikebana art involves the elimination of all but the essentials and thus requires trimming of branches and leaves. Beginners tend to be timid about this and neglect to trim material. But, in order to train your eye to the point of instantly knowing when to cut, it won't do to be afraid to trim. Developing

skill at trimming is one of the shortcuts to mastery of ikebana. Before people learn to make perfect omelets, they usually turn out some scorched ones. Similarly, in ikebana, beginners may trim a branch bare a few times, but it is just part of the learning process.

3. Scrupulously apply the basic techniques.

The basic techniques of cutting and setting flowers in the container, as well as bending material and conserving water, should be applied exactly as you have learned them. After these techniques have been learned, some people tend to grow negligent, but since ikebana is founded on the basis of these techniques, once skill has been acquired, the techniques should be applied at all times. Then, progress toward better arrangements is made more quickly.

4. Give thought to arrangements by others.

62

Utilize the chance to see ikebana made by others whenever you can. Although you may not understand much at first, you will be training yourself to appreciate ikebana. Try to grasp the vital points as if you were making the arrangement. Consider which flowers are used, how they are used, how they harmonize with the container, their dimensions, and so on.

5. Learn with the idea of teaching others.

Whether learning from a teacher or from this book, if you study with the idea of teaching another person soon after, learning will become a surprisingly rapid process. Learn with the idea that you have to teach it all to someone else. Practice with this in mind. If you do not, it will be to your own detriment.

6. Do not miss the chance to use seasonal flowers.

The seasons steadily change, and with them, the appropriate seasonal flowers. If you interrupt your training, you may miss the chance to use material at the time when it has the most appeal. If it is impossible to steadily continue practicing, at least continue to pay attention to the flowers of the seasons.

7. Think of good color combinations.

It is a human characteristic to like things which are beautiful. Women, especially, have an eye for well-designed things, and this can be extended to include ikebana. It is a matter of thinking of combining flowers with flowers, and flowers with containers, colors, and forms. With the mastery of this type of thinking, you will be able to easily express your ideas in the form of ikebana.

CHAPTER 3

AN UPRIGHT *MORIBANA* ARRANGEMENT
Pictured is a simple *moribana* arrangement of pear boughs and roses held by a frog in a basin. This type of arrangement is probably the most frequently used for everyday ikebana. Positioning the material in a corner makes optimum use of the space of the arrangement, which has the erect pear boughs as the 3 main stems and the roses as the 'assistant.'

MORIBANA ARRANGEMENTS

METHODS AND EXAMPLES

In ikebana, the distinction between *moribana* and *nage-ire-bana*, (*nage-ire*) can be generally seen in the kinds of containers used. Basins are used for *moribana* and vases for *nage-ire*, but the the methods of arrangement are also different.

Moribana is so named because an arrangement in the wide-mouthed, shallow container suggests that the arrangement is a serving (*moru* in Japanese means 'to serve up,' and is generally used on the occasion of filling a rice bowl, salad bowl, etc.). Flowers are held in the container by the metal frog.

Shown as an example is a classic *moribana* arrangement of water lilies, representing a waterside tableau.

CONCERNING *MORIBANA* CONTAINERS

Wide-mouthed basins are the classic containers for *moribana* and may be circular, square or rectangular. Boat-shaped containers and compotes with legs are also used for *moribana*. There are many unusual con-

tainers available, as well as those with decorations or patterns, but in the beginning, avoid elaborate or colorful containers and stick to simple ones. Because the flowers are beautiful, the container may be plain.

Porcelain is the commonest material for containers, but depending on the season and the arranger's intentions, wicker, bamboo, glass and sometimes copper or containers of other materials are used. Also, salad bowls, candy dishes, baskets and other vessels which are used in daily life are often used as ikebana containers.

1. Boat-shaped container with legs.
2. Freestyle compote.
3. Compote.
4. Candy basket used as a container.

The Positioning of the Container

Containers are, of course, essential to every flower arrangement. They are not merely to hold water, but also to harmonize with and complement the flowers they hold. Therefore, consideration must be given to the form of the container and its intended location.

Except for circular containers, which could be said to be the same from any angle, the position of the container with respect to the viewer can completely govern the feeling of the arranged flowers. If the container has some decoration, ears, legs, or a modified shape, a slight change in position produces a subtle change in the feeling and appeal of the arrangement. Thus, the effect that the position of the container will have on the arrangement must be considered when arranging.

Let us compare the different feelings or moods produced by the same arrangement in a fan-shaped basin when the basin is used in 2 positions. The materials are *sasa* bamboo, lily and chrysanthemum. Placed with the short side of the container forward, the arrangement is given a quiet, introspective air, but when the container is reversed the flowers appear livelier, more assertive. You can easily see how the 2 arrangements differ because of the position of the container.

Placing and Using the Frog

The frog which holds flowers and branches in place is an important tool in making *moribana* arrangements, but it is not a question of

just sticking the material into the frog—there are a number of processes involved.

The weight of the frog keeps the finished arrangement from falling over, but the position of the frog in the container is of great importance.

Whether the container is a compote with a narrowish mouth, a bowl, or a wide-mouthed basin, the position of the frog can greatly change the appearance of the finished arrangement. Let us see what it is like to use a rectangular frog.

Where to place the frog

With wide-mouthed basins and similar containers, when positioning the frog, provided there is no reason to do otherwise, avoid the middle and use one of the corners. This

practice has the following benefits: (a) the container is most fully utilized, (b) space is fully utilized, and (c) the three-dimensional relationship between the flowers and the container is most fully exploited. This is true for both types of frogs.

Just because the mouth of a container is wide does not mean the container should be filled with flowers; ikebana design and composition call for placing material in one spot and leaving the rest open, thus emphasizing and imparting strength to the material used.

Keeping the frog from slipping

Since porcelain and glass containers are frequently used, a little pressure on the metal frog will cause it to slide over the smooth surface. Just cut a piece of newspaper, or

any other material, to the same size as the frog, and place it underneath; the frog then will not slip.

How to use the frog

Rectangular frogs are generally used lengthwise, with a short side facing front (1). This is done so that even heavy branches which extend toward the front won't cause the arrangement to tip over. This placement is much stronger than when the frog is placed with the long side to the front.

The sun-and-moon frog is placed so that the round frog is to the front and the moon-shaped frog is to the rear (2). The principle is the same as for the rectangular frog.

Material is then fixed into the frog's pins, from the front half progressing to the back.

1

2

By doing this, the frog itself is thus easily concealed by the plant materials. However, when arranging a heavy branch, it is better to use the back half first.

Use the round part of the sun-and-moon frog first, and then the moon-shaped part. But always use the round one for heavy material.

Generally, rectangular frogs are placed lengthwise, but according to the materials used, various changes are made. For example, when heavy material is to be placed at an angle to the right, the frog's long side should lie obliquely, to the left (p. 73, [3]). Thus, conditions imposed by the materials often take precedence in placing the frog.

Combining frogs for added weight

When it seems as if a heavy branch set in a sun-and-moon frog might fall over, 2 moon-shaped frogs may be used, one added as a counterweight in the direction opposite to that of the branch.

In this case, hold the crescent frog upside down, with the concave side forward, as in photo (1), and nestle the crescent frog into

74

place on the round frog as in photo (2). The combined weight of the 2 frogs will keep the branch from falling. Just to lean the second frog against the first is not effective enough. This method of course can also be used for other frogs.

The position of the frog can greatly change the aspect of the finished arrangement. It was mentioned that the frog should be placed toward one of the corners of a basin, but what are the principles whereby the position can be determined?

Placing the frog to the right or left is determined by the nature of the materials and the place where the arrangement is to be displayed, while determining whether it is to be to the front or rear is dependent on the season.

Frogs are placed to the rear in summer and to the front in winter. In the case of basins, if the frog is placed to the front, the water is not visible, the appearance is not as refreshing, and the effect is more appropriate to winter than summer.

Both water and flowers are used together as materials, and for summer arrangements, whether the water is visible determines the difference between a lively arrangement and one lacking spirit.

This manner of thinking, calling for placing the frog so that the remaining space is used to good advantage, is also extended to basins, compotes and bowls.

In spring and autumn the position of the frog should relate to the proximity of summer or winter. The photos (p. 74) show arrangements of pine and chrysanthemum for winter (above) and summer (below).

HOW TO INSERT MATERIAL INTO A FROG
Although it looks easy to insert branches and stems into the frog, at first it may prove difficult. The method of inserting material varies according to the type of material.

When appraising an arrangement, an importance similar to that given to the appearance of the flowers should be given to the way the material has been inserted in the frog.

Insert herbaceous material immediately after trimming the stem
Ordinary flowers such as chrysanthemums and dahlias are inserted immediately after the stems are trimmed by cutting them straight across (1). Push them to the bottom of the frog (2).

3

4

5

6

Insert pencil-thick branches between the pins
As mentioned, branches about as thick as a pencil are cut to a tapering point (3). Insert the point of the tip between the frog's pins and press the branch until the tip reaches the bottom (4). Beginners often think it enough just to press the branch down, but it is much easier if done as suggested. And the larger surface resulting from the slanting cut means that more pins can penetrate the wood to hold the branch firmly.

Wrap thin stems and branches in paper before inserting
Thin stems of plants such as Chinese bell-flower and pinks, and even thin branches, are too thin to be held by or between pins. In such cases, wrap the bottom $\frac{1}{2}$ to one inch of the material in newspaper (5) and then insert between the pins, holding the wrapped portion as you push (6).

Inserting thick branches
Branches thicker than a pencil cannot be in-

serted between the pins. Therefore, cut straight across the bottom ¼ inch of the tapered end of the branch (7), and slit the cut end longitudinally. The thicker the branch, the more slits are needed. The branch can then be inserted easily, working it to the left and right while pushing (8).

Brace flowers which bend over

Flowers such as some lilies, and carnations, are too heavy for the stems to stand upright, and tend to bend over when held by the frog. Further, the stems of such flowers break easily. In such cases, tie a 3-inch piece of twig or stalk (9) to the bottom of the stem (10), using string or florist's wire. This twig or stalk should be of pencil thickness. (Keep a few ready together with your tools.) Press the branch into the frog (11).

Propping material to be inserted at an angle

When inserting material other than branches into a frog at an angle, the weakness of the stem presents a problem. Such material can

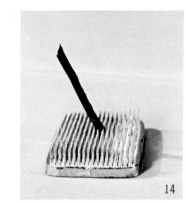

12

13

14

15

be supported by using a small branch as a prop.

To do this, cut a short pencil-thick branch and insert it into the frog as shown (12), having first cut the branch top at an angle so that the stem can easily be leaned on it. The height of the prop used varies according to the angle at which the material is to be set. Insert the material (here, gentian) and rest it on the prop, adjusting the prop to the desired angle (13).

Impale hollow-stemmed flowers on a twig

Flowers such as amaryllis and dahlia, with thick but hollow stems, cannot be inserted into a frog in the usual way because the bases of such stems are weak. When arranging such material, first prepare a 4-inch length of a branch of pencil thickness and insert it at about the angle desired for the material (14). Slide the hollow stem (here that of a dahlia) over the branch (15). Since it is difficult to change the angle after the stem has been inserted over the branch, try to set the branch as close to the desired angle as possible.

1

2

3

4

Moribana Practice
Upright arrangements

Let us try making a *moribana* arrangement of the popular upright pattern, using an azalea branch, 2 lilies and 2 lilac branches in a rectangular basin.

1. Here is how the material looks before trimming.

2. Trim the azalea as shown, leaving the central branch, to obtain the medium-length stem of the arrangement.

3. Trim the other side branch for use as the shortest of the 3 main stems. The central branch will be used as the arrangement's longest stem.

4. Having trimmed the 3 main branches, trim the other material also. Cut them to lengths somewhat longer than the intended final lengths to allow leeway while arranging. Trim the lower leaves from the lilies and lilacs.

5. Place the frog near the forward right corner of the container.

5

6. Cut the longest azalea branch to about 1½ times the container's width plus height, and insert it about 15 degrees off the vertical.

7. Trim any imperfect flowers and twig stubs from the medium-length branch. Do the same for the other 2 azalea branches.

8. Cut the medium-length branch to ⅔ the length of the longest one and set it at a 45 degree angle, toward the left.

9. Cut the shortest branch to ⅓ the length of the longest and arrange it so that it faces front, at about 60 degrees. This completes the arrangement of the body's framework.

10. The main stems now form an inverted pyramid; but before arranging the lilies and lilacs, carefully consider the balance between the pyramid and the container. Place a lily so that it occupies the central space between the azalea branches. It should be slightly longer than the shortest azalea branch.

11. Next, place the other lily to the left and in front of the medium-length branch. The lilies of the arrangement's 'assistant' have now been arranged, their white color making a fine contrast with the red of the azaleas.

12. With just the body and the lilies the arrangement does not yet have a delicate feeling. By putting a short white lilac branch in front of the long azalea branch, we make the azalea seem even redder.

13. Arrange the other lilac, slightly longer than the first, to the rear, completing the arrangement. The 3 main stems, azaleas, form the body of the arrangement and the lilies and lilacs harmoniously supplement them as the 'assistant.' Both the lilies and

lilacs are white, the former clear, the latter delicate, and together they function as contrasts to the azaleas.

14. This is the left view. You can see how all branches and flowers have been arranged so as to lean forward. The arrangement, of course, is properly viewed only from the front.

It is a basic ikebana rule to arrange material so that it leans to the front. This is to give the arrangement more depth than could be obtained if the material were arranged vertically.

15. Viewed from above, the left-right orientation of the material is easily seen.

16. Here the materials used are arrayed with the main branches in the center. The proportionate lengths of the main stems, as well as the supplementary material, can be readily seen, and you can see how the material differs from the way it was at the start.

MORIBANA MISCELLANEA 1
Using stones

Ikebana, and especially *moribana*, has traditionally aimed at the representation of natural scenes. The glorious, infinitely varied scenes of nature have served as models for ikebana. Thus, stones as well are sometimes incorporated into arrangements.

Stones are treated, like water, as ikebana material. Generally, when stones are used, an open area of water also should be visible in the arrangement.

Here, stones tumbled and worn smooth by the waters of a river form the main axis of a *moribana* arrangement. The ample presence of water lends refreshment to the arrangement. The bamboo is tall, but light, and with the daisies, lower and heavier in the feeling they impart in this arrangement, an exquisitely unified combination is achieved.

16

The pebbles scattered in the basin also contribute to the arrangement's effectiveness.

MORIBANA MISCELLANEA 2
Arranging fruit in a basket

If only conventional containers are used, and flowers arranged strictly according to form, ikebana loses its life and interest. Therefore, ikebana includes provisions for the use of containers originally meant for other purposes.

This basket is a kind commonly used in Japanese kitchens to hold vegetables, but here has been used with a *moribana* arrangement of dahlias and chestnuts. Since water cannot be added to this type of container, a small glass or jar, to which the frog and water are added, is used inside the basket. For the sake of the arrangement's harmony and composition, one chestnut sprig has been placed outside the basket, a common technique to assure that the branch and nut or fruit used in the arrange-

ment are clearly visible. The chestnuts are considered equivalent to flowers in designing this type of arrangement.

MORIBANA MISCELLANEA 3
Using compotes

Compotes, or fruit bowls, are available in many forms, and are equally adaptable for practice arrangements or arrangements made to decorate the home.

The spirea arranged in a compote here is a cascading *moribana* arrangement.

Although *moribana* containers are generally low, requiring that cascading arrangements be displayed on a shelf, this is not necessary when a tall container such as this is used.

MORIBANA MISCELLANEA 4
Using foliage in a bowl

Plant materials have color and form, and impart their individual feeling. Branches may

83

be rough or gentle in texture, harsh or soft in color. The purple and pink cornflowers used in this arrangement evoke a 'sweet' mood and are coupled with the fatsia, which has clear-cut form, resulting in an interesting contrast. The horizontal stripes of the container unite the 2 types of plants used.

This type of container may be used for either *moribana* or *nage-ire* arrangements. For *nage-ire* arrangements, a tall thin vase can be inserted in such a container, and water and plant materials inserted into that, while for a *moribana* arrangement, sand or pebbles can be added to the container, making it shallow, and a frog can be placed on the sand. If the container were not so deep, the frog could be placed on the bottom without the use of sand.

This arrangement can be considered a modern *moribana* arrangement.

Moribana Miscellanea 5
Using glass containers

As in the previous example, when arranging with a container which is deep or has a bottom which is not level, small stones can be placed in the container to make a new, level bottom on which to place the frog. After the frog is firmly in place, the flowers can be arranged.

For this arrangement, using a glass compote and evening mist and bulrush, the material cannot be arranged directly on the bottom

84

because the frog cannot be stabilized. After placing some stones in the compote, the arrangement can be made. The transparency of the glass gives the container a fresh, cool appearance.

This arrangement effects a fine contrast by using the straight lines of the bulrush in a radiating form and the evening mist as masses at different levels above the container. The purple of the evening mist is richly reflected by the container.

MORIBANA MISCELLANEA 6
The pleasure and charm of compound arrangements

Ikebana containers are not necessarily limited to only one opening into which material can be inserted. Many containers have 2 openings, but are used for a single arrangement. Basins and other containers with broad bases may have 3 or 4 openings, and even these can be used for a single beautifully composed arrangement.

There are also instances when 2 separate arrangements are made—in 2 containers —and then combined to make one ikebana composition.

In general terms arrangements using a container with more than one opening or using more than one container are called compound arrangements. Some compound arrangements are made by combining *moribana* and *nage-ire* arrangements. All qualities of ikebana—color combinations, forms, containers —are multiplied in compound arrangements, leading to greater enjoyment.

However, it must be understood that in compound arrangements it is necessary that a number of elements be composed together, organically, as one creation. One must not merely bring many flowers together.

Let us look at some examples.

A modern compound arrangement

This arrangement of poppies and purple and yellow tulips in a Dutch plate serves to illustrate how groupings of flowers can be composed in a single container.

Tulips should be arranged no more than 30 degrees off the vertical as they show a strong tendency to face the sun when growing, standing erect without nodding toward the ground.

Placing the container at an angle gives it a modern design feeling. This type of arrangement can also be used for a container with 2 openings, in which case the tulips are inserted in one opening and the poppies in the other.

85

Blending red and white chrysanthemums

This arrangement, made by using 2 salad bowls and 7 red and white chrysanthemums, is an example of how you can make a compound arrangement with 2 containers.

The most important idea in composing compound arrangements is the esthetic relationships of the elements. Here, the characteristic beauty of the stems' straight lines, blending with one another and crowned by the red and white flowers, forms an interesting and unified brocade.

In this arrangement, if one looks at only one container, the chrysanthemums seem extremely long in relation to the bowls, as if unbalanced. However, when you realize that the key factor is the total dimensions of both bowls, it becomes clear that there is balance, and that the chrysanthemums are of the required length. When 2 containers are used for a compound arrangement, the length of the material must be determined on the basis of the total dimensions of both containers.

Chrysanthemums are usually used in erect form, giving a peaceful mood to the arrangement, but here is an example of ikebana where they are used to create a lively atmosphere. Chrysanthemums of the same size but different color can be used in this way, cut to proportional lengths, or small and large chrysanthemums of the same color can be arranged. The former will result in a colorful, even gaudy, arrangement, while the latter will convey a mood of sophistication.

Placing one container atop another

Containers may be stacked or stepped, as has been done with these round trays. The

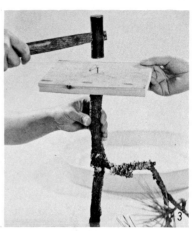

composition consists of a red rose in the lower tray and a red rose and yellow narcissus in the upper tray. The black lacquer interior of the trays makes an effective contrast with the striped exterior. A little water has been added to the trays, and small frogs are used.

Compound arrangements can thus show variety in the placement of containers in this way as well.

MORIBANA MISCELLANEA 7
Using branches in moribana arrangements
There is a special way of holding branches in place for *moribana* arrangements; it is often used when arranging a branch so large that it would fall over if held only by a frog. Pine branches used for ikebana are often thick, so they are fastened to a board. In Japan, this is often done for arrangements in the New

Year season, when pine is one of the favorite materials for ikebana.

The ikebana shown, of a pine branch and roses, is considered especially appropriate to the New Year.

The pine is valued for its evergreen qualities, and since antiquity has been considered symbolic of longevity. The rose, the queen of flowers, has similarly been valued from ancient times; in China it acquired the name 'long spring' because it well represents the tranquility and cheerfulness of spring. In the Orient, the combination of pine and rose, symbolizing both long life and spring, has thus often been used as a theme of paintings.

To fix the pine branch in place, obtain a board about 6 by 8 by $\frac{1}{2}$ inches; wood from a fruit crate is one possible source. The wood need not be smooth and free from blemishes.

4

5

6

7

1 (p. 87). Before anything else, determine the angle at which the branch is to be used and its height in the finished arrangement. Determine the angle and the place where the branch will be cut very carefully, as it will be difficult, at best, to change them later.

2 (p. 87). With a saw, cut according to your estimate for the length and angle of the branch.

3 (p. 87). Holding the branch upside down, attach the board by driving a nail through the board into the branch. Have someone help you with this step. You will have no trouble centering both nail and branch; if 2 diagonals are drawn on the board from corner to corner with a pencil, they will intersect at the center. It is also helpful to start a hole in advance, before the nail is actually driven.

4. Carefully adjust the branch to the correct angle.

5. Place the board in the container and place a large rectangular frog on top of it. Insert the first pink rose.

6. Insert the remaining yellow and pink roses. (Side view from above)

7. Scatter pebbles or sand in the bottom to fully conceal the board and frog, add some water, and the arrangement is completed.

1

2

3

4

MORIBANA MISCELLANEA 8
'Washed-roots' moribana

This form of *moribana* uses plants with roots which have been washed, instead of cut flowers. Potted plants, such as primrose, cineraria and cyclamen, would have to be thrown away later if they were cut for ikebana use, but using this method enables one to appreciate them for a short while in a flower arrangement and then return them to the pot. Although this method can be used for garden plants or foliage plants, mostly it is used for potted plants.

In this example, potted cineraria and lily have been combined for a *moribana* arrangement in a decorative open-weave basket. An empty can or jar is used to hold water and the frog.

1. Remove the entire plant from its pot and gently shake all loose soil from the roots.

2. Wash the remaining soil off by immersing the roots several times in a bowl of water.

3. Place the frog in the can, and cut a

5

pencil-thick branch to a 3½-inch length and insert it in the frog.

4. Insert the cineraria, with roots, into the can, and having determined the angle at which it is to be set, tie it to the branch for support. Cut off and discard any extra portion of the branch.

5. Determine the length of the lilies and insert them into the frog so that they balance the cineraria in the arrangement's composition.

MORIBANA MISCELLANEA 9
Floating flowers

Arrangements of flowers floating on the surface of water can be made only in the *moribana* style. The refreshing feeling imparted by 2 or 3 flowers floating on the water of a wide compote or basin is perceived at a glance, and this type of arrangement is naturally best suited for summer. It is often used as a centerpiece on parlor or dining room tables.

The flowers used must be refreshing in appearance, but may previously have been used in another arrangement.

Combining flowers and leaves

When arranging floating flowers, all but a short stub of the stem should be cut. Leaves can then be tied to this stub, which should be as long as the water in the container is deep (1), (2).

Evergreen magnolia leaves have been tied to

a lily, and the combination has been placed in a cut glass salad bowl (3). Leaving the stem this long will tend to keep the flower in one place, but if you wish the flowers to float freely, the trick is simply to cut the stem shorter so that it does not reach the bottom. This has been done with chrysanthemums in the example shown above.

Piercing leaves with the flower stem

Floating flower arrangements often utilize colorful flowers such as chrysanthemums, dahlias, lilies, hydrangeas and water lilies. In these cases, the stub of the flower stem is pressed through the leaf or leaves used, as shown above. The foliage then provides a background for the flowers. Hydrangea leaves were combined with chrysanthemums for this arrangement in a compote. Interest is provided by the unusual combination of the 2 plants.

MORIBANA MISCELLANEA 10

Holding material with stones

Moribana arrangements can be made with stones which both hold the plant material in place and simultaneously form part of the composition. This is an old, uniquely Japanese, idea.

Here, lilies have been matched with evening mist and stones in a nearly flat ceramic container, resulting in a quiet, refined ikebana.

Some stones prop the flowers at the desired angle while others are used to hold the flowers in place. All elements are harmoniously combined in a restrained arrangement.

CHAPTER 4

A Spreading *Nage-ire* Arrangement
Narrow-mouthed, tall containers are characteristic of
nage-ire, as is the use of a simple device rather than a
frog to hold the material in place. This casual-looking
arrangement of sweet sultan and allium serves to bring
out the natural qualities of the flowers, with the humor-
ous ball-shaped burr of the allium contrasting well
with the sprightly sweet sultan. The whole provides
a musical mood due to the rhythms of each, resulting
in a modern arrangement in the spreading pattern.

NAGE-IRE ARRANGEMENTS

What Is *Nage-ire*?

Nage-ire, or *nage-ire-bana*, is an ikebana style using narrow-mouthed, tall containers, into which flowers appear to have been literally 'thrown' or dropped. Long popular, this style uses plant materials in their natural state, in containers such as those made of bamboo, or in water pitchers. Frogs are not used to hold the flowers. Instead, simple devices are made and fitted to either the material or container. Thus, this style and *moribana* differ in respect to the containers used and the method of holding material in place.

The photo shows a classic *nage-ire* arrangement of a rose and flowering peach branch, made in an instant using a fresh green bamboo container.

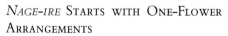

1

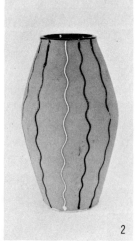

2

NAGE-IRE STARTS WITH ONE-FLOWER ARRANGEMENTS

Not all *nage-ire* arrangements require a device to hold material.

We often cut a garden flower and simply place it in a cup; this too is *nage-ire*. We can say that *nage-ire* starts with one-flower arrangements such as these. The basic beauty of *nage-ire* arrangements is present even in such simple arrangements.

Although it is often thought that the narrow-mouthed, tall flower vases and pitchers used in *nage-ire* show less variation than *moribana* containers, we often find unusual containers usable for *nage-ire*.

Nage-ire arrangements are based on a special respect for the naturalness of flowers and their harmonious combination with the container, thus making the container an especially vital element. These containers can be broadly divided into 3 categories: cylinders, bowls, and pitchers or jars.

The photo illustrates a one-flower arrangement of magnolia in a ceramic jar.

CONCERNING NAGE-IRE CONTAINERS

The most commonly used container for *nage-ire* is the cylindrical vase, a tall container with a mouth that is not very wide and sides that are nearly vertical. *Nage-ire* vases may be round, square or hexagonal, broad at the base or with protruding shoulders. They may be ceramic, bamboo, or metal, or of other materials, but for beginners a cylindrical container without decoration is recommended.

bowls can only be used for *moribana* arrangements. Deep bowls with mouths that are not wide can be used for *nage-ire* arrangements.

HOLDING MATERIAL IN PLACE: *NAGE-IRE* METHODS

There are a number of devices that can be used for either containers or plant materials to hold the materials in place in *nage-ire* arrangements. Such methods enable the arranger to place branches and flowers in any direction or angle desired. The ways of holding material in place are divided according to the device or method used, as follows:

(1) No device is used; the material stays in place of its own accord.

(2) Half-Moon Method. A bow-shaped twig is fitted in the container to hold the material in place.

(3) Cross Support Method. A cross made by tying branches together at right angles is placed in the container.

(4) Vertical and Horizontal Supports. In the case of woody material, the base is split and a short twig is inserted, forming a foot-like appendage, thus bracing the material in the container.

(5) Tripod. By tying the material a few inches from the bottom of the stems and then separating 3 stems as the legs of a tripod, the entire arrangement can be made to rest steadily.

(6) Jumbled Wire. Jumble wire into an open mass, place it in the container and merely set the material in the wire.

Photo (1) shows a pestle-shaped *nage-ire* vase; photo (2), a modified vase.

Nage-ire containers can add greatly to arrangements and can considerably augment the beauty of the flowers used. The gentle feeling evoked by a round container, the feeling of stability evoked by a broad-based container—all this can help set off the beauty of the flowers.

However, it is very difficult to hold materials in place in a jar without frogs, unless some kind of supports are used. Furthermore, mastery of methods of holding materials in *nage-ire* arrangements is especially necessary when the container is wide-mouthed like the one in photo (4).

Bowl-shaped containers come in a variety of forms, but the shallow, wide-mouthed

the back of the glass. Since the second rose is to lean toward the right, its stem is braced against the left, inside the glass. The stems cross, and the stem of the first rose placed in the glass is also held down by the stem of the second.

Half-Moon Method

When the above method is not sufficient, or, for that matter, for all *nage-ire* arrangements, after the arranging is completed, a short twig, bent like a bow, is inserted in the container from behind and placed near the top. It stays in place and holds the material in the container due to its tension. The slightly arched twig and round wall of the container form a halfmoon, hence the name of this method.

The photo below shows the arrangement of 2 roses with a slightly arched twig inserted in the glass; basically, this is how the half-moon method looks. The twig should be somewhat thinner than a pencil. Willow twigs are often used. It can be a little longer

Arranging Roses Without Any Device

When no device is used, the material is supported by its own strength and by the container itself in the position it is placed. The bottom of the stem or branch is in contact with the bottom of the container and the stem leans against the lip.

Shown is a casual *nage-ire* arrangement of yellow roses in the simplest of all containers, a glass. The first rose is placed facing front with the bottom of the stem braced against

or shorter than the diameter of the container's mouth, depending on the container, on whether a large number of materials have been used, or on whether branches are included in the arrangement.

CROSS SUPPORT METHOD
A slanting arrangement of flowering pear boughs and lilies

The pear tree, like the plum, peach and cherry, flowers before the leaves appear in spring. After cutting the branch under water, the base of it is to be split before it is put in the container. The orange-colored lilies should also be cut under water.

1. Cut a pencil-thick twig, slightly longer than the diameter of the container's mouth.

2. Insert it at an angle, as shown, with one end of the twig $\frac{1}{4}$ inch from the top.

3. Raise the lower end of the twig until it fits tightly, $\frac{1}{4}$ inch from the top.

4. Cut another twig and insert it below the first in the same way.

5. Turn the container so that the twigs, when facing front, form the letter 'X'. Fill the container with water to the top of the twigs. The water will cause the twigs to expand and hold firmly against the walls of the container.

6. Determine the length of the longest pear branch (according to the dimensions of the container) and its position in the finished arrangement.

7. Since this branch looks a bit crowded, trim part of it, obtaining at the same time the medium-length branch.

8. Having cut off what will be the medium-length branch, use that which remains as the longest branch. It is $1\frac{1}{2}$ times the height plus width of the container.

9. Arrange the long branch so it forms a

rear mass in the arrangement, leaning to the left and front.

10. Arrange the medium-length branch in the rear, leaning to the right and front.

11. From the side, one can see how the cut ends of the branches are touching the container and are supported by the cross.

12. Cut the remaining branch at the fork and use the most attractive part as the short branch. Trim as necessary and cut it to $\frac{1}{3}$ the length of the longest branch.

13. Using it to the front, place the short branch so that the stem is under the cross and the base of the stem touches the rear of the container. Arrange it to the left and about at water level.

14. Having finished the body of the arrangement, prepare the lilies for use as the 'assistant.' Keep the leaves and flowers dry, because if they get wet they will rot.

15. Cut this lily somewhat short and arrange it low and to the front.

16. Cut the leaves from the second lily and leave it a bit longer than the first. Place it in the center, higher than the first, and leaning front. Both lilies have been arranged to the front. This photo, taken from the side, shows the length, direction, angles and placement of the material.

17, 18. To hold the long and medium branches more firmly, add a single twig (as a halfmoon support) to the container, behind the material, bending it like a bow so that it is tight within the container and presses against the material.

19. This is the finished arrangement, seen from the front.

1

2

19

Horizontal Support
Arranging rhododendrons and asters

This method involves adding a device to the material and then arranging the material in the container. The 2 methods, horizontal and vertical, are both frequently used, and sometimes are combined.

Rhododendrons may look beautiful from one angle, but from another angle they may not appear attractive. One has to determine which angle enables the flowers to appear most beautiful.

1. Considering the nature of this branch, it should be arranged this way.

2. If simply placed in the vase, it will fall over like this. Some technique must be used to keep it in the desired position.

3. Cut the base of the branch in order to insert a twig as a support. Trim the tip of the branch first. Use the scissors as a lever while cutting, and cut deeply.

4. Cut a twig of pencil thickness to be a

little shorter than the diameter of the vase's mouth, and insert it fairly deeply in the split of the branch, so that it is held firmly in place.

5. If the twig is still unsteady, tie it with string or wire.

6. Insert the branch in the vase at the desired angle. The twig should be in firm contact with both sides of the vase, a little to the rear; it was cut a little short for off-center placement. The photo shows a side view.

7. The rhododendron is in place as planned.

8. Place a second rhododendron so as to lean to the left, resting it against the twig.

9. Arrange the asters between the rhododendron branches, forming the 'assistant,' and the arrangement is complete.

This is a variation of a slanting arrangement.

1

2

9

VERTICAL SUPPORT

Combining evergreen magnolia with chrysanthemum

Let's try a *nage-ire* arrangement using the vertical support device. For containers which tend to be spherical in shape, horizontal supports can be easily used, but for the type of container pictured here with a narrow neck, a vertical support is best used.

A *nage-ire* arrangement of evergreen magnolia placed so as to project out to the left, and with contrasting chrysanthemums placed in the center and leaning to the right, is shown here (photo of finished arrangement, p. 109). This ikebana harmonizes well with the vertically-striped container.

1. The magnolia is to be placed so as to project to the left in a rising arc.

2. If inserted without any support, it will just fall over. The flowers and leaves should under no circumstances face the rear.

3. Having decided at what angle and direction to set the branch, cut it to the

107

proper length in relation to the container. The cut should be oblique. Split the base of the branch by cutting with the scissors.

4. Cut a twig somewhat thicker than a pencil to a length about 3 inches longer than the depth of the container. Fit it into the split of the branch as shown.

5. Tie the branch and twig.

6. Cut the attached twig to the proper length so that it will fit in the container and, while touching bottom, hold the branch at the right height.

A word of caution: Both ends of branches used as vertical supports must touch the inside of the container, at the bottom and near the shoulder, so when cutting it to the proper length, cut short sections at a time to insure that you won't make it too short to be used.

7. Having cut it to the proper length, insert it in the container.

8. The magnolia branch is now held in place at the desired angle and in the desired direction.

Once this technique has been learned, you will be able to arrange even heavy branches

in such a way that a considerable jolt will not cause them to fall out of position. After this branch is in place, the rest is easy.

9. Arrange 5 chrysanthemums, leaning them on the solidly placed magnolia branch, and paying attention to their differences in length as they are arranged. The photo shows the finished arrangement.

Leaves of plants such as the evergreen magnolia are often relatively too large for many arrangements; in such cases it is permissible to trim the leaves to a more reasonable size, taking care that the form of the leaf is not altered.

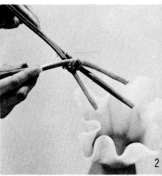

TRIPOD METHOD
Arranging gladiolus in a glass container

The tripod method is used when other methods are difficult to apply because of the configuration of the container, or for a glass container. As is suggested by its name, this method involves spreading a few stems apart for support below a point where they have been tied together.

Since several of the stems must be spread, this method cannot be used for narrow containers. It can be used, however, for wide-mouthed bowls or jars or other unusual containers.

This is the best method when the surface of the container is slippery, or when the stems are slippery such as is the case with gladiolus and amaryllis.

This arrangement uses 3 gladiolus cut to different lengths, and a glass container.

1. Having already determined the lengths of the flowers and their directions, tie them

3

4

5

together at a point from their ends somewhat less than the height of the container and spread the respective stems below the tied point in the direction opposite to the one intended for the flowers.

2. Adjust the directions of the stems and place the material in the container.

3. Seen from above, the ends of the stems rest against the bottom of the container.

4. A front view. The material has been adjusted; the composition of this standing arrangement is now clear.

5. The 'assistant' gladiolus and leaves have been added.

This is how the tripod method works; it can also be used for 'assistant' material. When arranging primroses, cyclamen and other flowers, this technique can be advantageously used. When combining such flowers, each variety can be tied separately and supported by its own tripod.

2

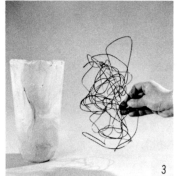

3

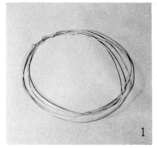

1

4

JUMBLED WIRE METHOD

Arranging 5 roses

All there is to this method is to jumble wire into an open mass and put the wire into the container. The flowers are then inserted in the wire mass.

As in the tripod method, this is used when a container does not lend itself readily to the use of a short support made from a branch, and is very useful for smooth-surfaced containers such as those made of glass. It is especially atttractive in that it is simple to make and use—anyone can easily jumble the wire as needed.

Sixteen-gauge wire should be used, at the rate of about one yard for about $\frac{1}{2}$ pint volume. The jumbled mass of wire can be reused many times.

First, let's start with the preparation of the wire.

1. This is what 16-gauge wire looks like.

5

2. Bend the wire at intervals about the same as the width of your palm.

3. The finished mass of wire should look roughly like this.

4. Insert it in the vase.

5. Insert the roses into the wire mass. The framework provided by the wire is so complicated that flowers can be inserted so as to rest in any position desired. This is how the roses rest in the wire mass.

6. The finished arrangement. A horizontal support made from a thin branch has been inserted in the container to provide added support.

6

NAGE-IRE MISCELLANEA 1

An upright arrangement in a tall rectangular container

Here is a standing arrangement of red-purple and white snapdragons in a 4-sided container which has protruding decorations.

When making standing arrangements in *nage-ire* style, if both the container and the material are tall, the total effect tends to be one of unbalance. Therefore, as was done in this example, the lower portion of the arrangement should be made more prominent. The snapdragons should be cut to the prescribed lengths for long, medium and short stems. Placing the container so that its decorations are to the sides also helps offset the relatively tall height of the arrangement. A single support, placed near the top of the container, will suffice to hold the material steady.

112

NAGE-IRE MISCELLANEA 2

A spreading arrangement in a ceramic jar

The peony is rightly called 'the king of flowers.' Here, it has been used for a *nage-ire* arrangement in an Italian jar. The curved lines of the added deutzia branches are used to form a spreading arrangement.

If the design of the jar is not well chosen, the container will overpower the placid beauty of the peony. To obtain balance, the deutzia branches are arranged to the left and right.

As in this example, when using containers such as this one, take care not to hide the container's form and decoration. Since the neck of the container is round, a cross support has been used.

NAGE-IRE MISCELLANEA 3

A wide-mouthed vase without added support

White columbine has been placed in this deep flare-lipped container from Persia, try-ing for a balance between dense and sparse placement of flowers of only one type.

NAGE-IRE MISCELLANEA 4

A cascading arrangement for a narrow-mouthed vase

Akebia, a climber, bears fruit from summer to autumn. Here its natural lines are used unchanged, in a cascading arrangement. Daisies have been gathered in a cluster just above the vase's mouth to contrast with the akebia. The daisies have been tied in a bundle in the tripod method. The vase's

is considered a most felicitious combination in Japan, and is often used for New Year's ikebana.

The pine is used as the long stem, the plum as the medium stem and the chrysanthemum as the short stem in this standing arrangement. Horizontal and vertical supports have been used.

NAGE-IRE MISCELLANEA 6
A compound arrangement in an unusual container
In this container having 2 mouths, pampas grass has been combined with a chrysanthemum and a branch with paulownia fruit to make a compound *nage-ire* arrangement. Compound arrangements are often used in *nage-ire*. Here, leaves, a flower and fruit are combined in a fitting autumn ikebana.

mouth is too narrow to permit the use of any other method; no device has been used.

NAGE-IRE MISCELLANEA 5
A cheerful arrangement of pine, plum and chrysanthemum
A classic *nage-ire* arrangement of pine, plum and chrysanthemum has been harmoniously placed in this jar. Pine symbolizes eternal youth due to its evergreen nature; plum, because it flowers despite cold weather, is revered by flower lovers; and chrysanthemum is even more of a favorite because of its fragrance and upright form. Together with the pine-bamboo-plum combination, this trio

CHAPTER 5

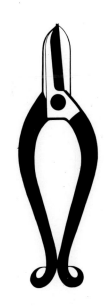

A Table Center

Until recently, there were virtually no instances of placing arranged flowers in the center of a room; ikebana was specifically made to adorn the *tokonoma* alcove or a wall. The Occidental style of placing flowers so that they can be seen from all sides started with the adoption of Occidental patterns of living in modern Japan.

The enjoyment of a centerpiece such as this one, when people are seated at a table to drink tea or enjoy a meal, is by no means monopolized by East or West. The arrangement here offers a bright combination of the orange color of the Kafir lilies and the white of the marguerites to delight the eye.

116

APPRECIATING IKEBANA

FROM ONE TO ALL DIRECTIONS

The side of an arrangement to be seen and appreciated is the side which appears most beautiful, or, in other words, the side arranged keeping in mind the direction from which the composition will be seen. Every arrangement invariably has such a side.

Until recently, the side of an arrangement to be appreciated has been limited to one, because ikebana developed within the con-fines of the *tokonoma* alcove of Japanese homes. Since feudal times, the *tokonoma* has been the spiritual center of Japanese homes, the place where scrolls, antiques, etc. were displayed. Although only a corner of one room, the *tokonoma* has played an important role in the formation of the style of Japanese residential architecture.

Virtually all flower arrangements were placed in the *tokonoma*, never in the center of

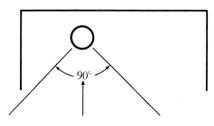

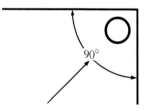

the room or in another corner of the house. If a house lacked a *tokonoma*, a shelf or low platform served as a substitute, above which scrolls would be hung and on which ikebana could be displayed.

Flowers in the *tokonoma* or on a shelf, due to the conditions imposed by the form and location of these places of display, appear most beautiful when seen from one direction—the front.

However, the Japanese way of living has changed completely. Japanese homes have been greatly modernized and the importance of the *tokonoma* has dwindled. Most important of all, ikebana is no longer limited to the *tokonoma*, but is now used to decorate any part of the house.

Ikebana is now placed in the living room, or on a table so that all those seated there may enjoy it. Simultaneous with the popularization of decorating tables with

ikebana has come the necessity to appreciate the arrangement from all sides.

ONE-DIRECTION IKEBANA
The most common form of ikebana used to liven up a room is the type which is appreciated from a single side. In modern homes there are many places which can be decorated with this kind of arrangement, and while we are getting further and further from the old traditions, this standard of beauty will probably be preserved, at least to some extent. Such arrangements, by and large,

are best viewed from within 45 degrees on either side of a point directly in front of the composition. The place may be before any wall that is not broad or in a corner, and this arrangement may be of the *moribana*, *nage-ire*, or any other style. Whether the arrangement is *moribana* or *nage-ire*, the 3 main stems should be cut to standard length.

TWO-DIRECTION IKEBANA

Two-direction ikebana, such as arrangements decorating a spot in front of a broad wall, are those which are appreciated from either side as well as from the front.

There are many occasions when this type can be used at home, in offices, stores and elsewhere. This type should be planned so as to be appreciated from within an arc of 180 degrees, and the main stems or branches should extend to a considerable length to the left or right so that the arrangement can be

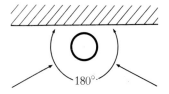

appreciated from either side. Further, in two-direction arrangements, the larger the 'assistant' the better.

Just because it is a two-direction arrangement does not mean that a greater variety and quantity of materials than in the case of one-direction arrangements must be included. Quantity is determined by the size and the requirements of the arrangement itself. In the same sense that there are times when much material is used in one-direction arrangements, in two-direction arrangements there are times to avoid using too little material. Two-direction arrangements may also be *moribana*, *nage-ire*, or any other style.

THREE-DIRECTION IKEBANA

Three-direction ikebana may be appreciated, of course, from the front and sides, and, to some extent, from the back as well. Such an arrangement presents a broad expanse of flowers for appreciation. This type of arrangement is best for places where there is considerable activity, such as a salon, lobby or meeting place, an outside corner, and in show windows.

Although often used in public and semi-public places, these arrangements sometimes also can be made for the home, if the place to be decorated is not too narrow.

This type of arrangement is made to be seen from within an arc of 270 degrees, so the finished arrangement must be quite large. The most important means of achieving this is by placing each of the main stems in a different direction. The directions and sizes

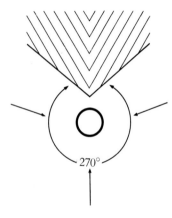

of the stems are determined by the nature of the materials and the place of the finished arrangement.

As one progresses from one- to two- and three-direction arrangements, the dimensions of materials used must be increased. All styles of arrangements, *moribana*, *nage-ire*, etc., can be made in the three-direction type.

122

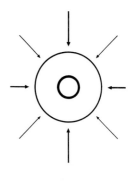

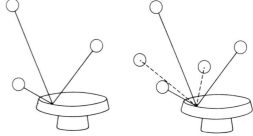

ALL-DIRECTION IKEBANA

All-direction ikebana comprises those arrangements decorating a parlor or dining room table, and can be seen from all sides. Celebrations, dinner parties and other gatherings provide good opportunities to use this type of arrangement. All-direction ikebana is the result of Western influence on patterns of living, and is now common in Japan. Of course, it has as many applications in the Occident as in Japan.

Because it is seen from all sides does not mean that much more material than used for a one-direction arrangement is needed. In practice, twice the amount needed for a one-direction ikebana is sufficient.

When arranging the main stems, place the medium and short stems in directions opposite to that of the long stem. Two stems each may be used for the medium and short stems

of the body, as shown in the diagram. To fill out the arrangement, double the amount of 'assistant' materials that would be used for a one-direction arrangement.

Furthermore, because these arrangements are designed to be seen from all sides, in this case only it is permissible to use a frog in the center of a round basin. The simplest form of an all-direction arrangement would be just a single flower arranged so as to be easily seen from above.

The main stems of an all-direction ikebana should be $\frac{1}{2}$ the standard stem lengths.

All-direction Ikebana Forms

The most typical styles of all-direction arrangements are the pyramid and the bowl. The stems of a pyramid-style arrangement resemble a standard slanting pattern made into an all-direction arrangement, and the bowl style resembles a standard spreading pattern made into an all-direction arrangement.

This disposition of materials is not limited to all-direction arrangements. Two- and three-direction arrangements also show upright, slanting, spreading, cascading or horizontal patterns depending on the disposition of the main stems.

In all-direction arrangements, however, the slanting and spreading patterns are most common. Cascading all-direction arrangements can also be made for places such as the very center of a hall or salon where an arrangement can be suspended from above.

1

Horizontal pattern arrangements, from the viewpoint of how they can be appreciated, are classic examples of all-direction arrangements.

The only type of ikebana which cannot be used for an all-direction arrangement is the type suspended from a wall.

Making an All-direction Arrangement

Now, let us make an all-direction arrangement. The materials used in the example given as a guide here are 10 chysanthemums and a compote. The finished ikebana is to be a slightly slanting, upright arrangement.

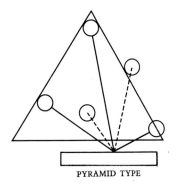

PYRAMID TYPE

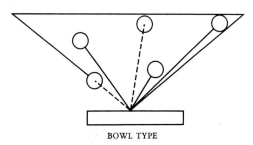

BOWL TYPE

124

3

4

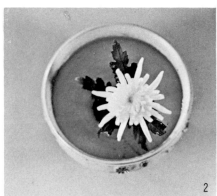

2

5

1. First, place the frog in the center. Cut the long stem a bit shorter than the usual standard length and arrange it a little obliquely and to the right.

2. This is how it should look from directly above.

3. Cut the medium stem to $\frac{2}{3}$ the length of the long stem.

4. Cut the short stem to $\frac{1}{3}$ the length of the longest and arrange it leaning to the left and front. The 3 chrysanthemums form a pyramid. Although the stems may be slightly short, this body does not differ at all from that of a one-direction arrangement.

5. Turn the container around, or work from the opposite side.

6. Working on this side, use the long

6

7

8

9

10

stem as it is and make a second medium stem, arranging it to lean to the left.

7. Place the second short stem to the right. The main stems total 5.

8. From the inital 'front' view, the stems are just opposite each other.

9. Here is the arrangement seen from above. These 5 main stems are insufficient, so add 5 more chrysanthemums, while turning the container, to form a harmonizing 'assistant.'

10. First, add a short chrysanthemum to the center, facing the 'back.'

11. This is the view from the 'back' at this stage.

12. In the 'front,' add a short chrysanthemum to the center, leaning to the 'front.'

13. This is the view from the 'back,' with 2 flowers added to the arrangement's body.

11

126

12

13

14

15

14. A flower slightly shorter than a medium stem is now added (from the 'front'), leaning to the right. Place leaves around the base, low, so as to conceal the frog. When working with materials which do not have leaves, prepare suitable substitute foliage for this purpose. Arrange a stem about as long as a medium chrysanthemum, leaning to the left. This fills out the left portion of the 'front.'

15. From the 'front,' add a flower, about the same length as one of the short chrysanthemums, to the 'back' and leaning to the right. Now, complete by adding the leaves, avoiding making the center too cluttered.

16. Here is the completed arrangement as seen from above. The chrysanthemums are displayed in all directions.

16

USING LILIES AND HEMP PALM LEAVES
In this example, orange lilies have been arranged in 3 directions and leaves of the hemp palm have been placed within this framework as the 'assistant.' The leaves are arranged to face all directions. A few smaller lilies are also included in the 'assistant.' As the neck of the container is narrow, no device has been used to hold the materials.

AN ALL-DIRECTION *NAGE-IRE* ARRANGEMENT
Usually, *moribana* is used for ikebana meant as a table center, but not all all-direction arrangements are *moribana* arrangements. *Nage-ire* arrangements are also possible. According to *nage-ire* methods, it is possible to use only 3 large flowers to make an all-direction arrangement. What is meant by 'large flowers' are roses, carnations, lilies, clematis, dahlias and herbaceous peonies. Using the lines of the flowers, leaves and stems, they are arranged in a complete circle of 360 degrees. Of course, the 'assistant' is appropriately added between the main branches.

128

USING ONLY 3 CLEMATIS

Interesting all-direction arrangements can be made with only 3 flowers.

Shown is a *nage-ire* arrangement of purple and white clematis, especially appropriate for brightening up an office.

The richness of the clematis works so well that there is no need for an 'assistant.' Also, since the clematis is a climber, its own stems can be used to support the flowers when placed in the container, and no special device is needed. However, a cross support can be used.

129

CHAPTER 6

ARRANGEMENTS HUNG FROM ABOVE OR FROM A WALL
These arrangements are especially notable for their graceful use of space.

Here is an appropriately light cascading *moribana* arrangement of pine, camellia and bittersweet in a three-cornered basket.

Dahlia and clematis have been used for this arrangement in a porcelain container hung on a pillar; it may be viewed from a wide angle. Note the similar forms of the petals of both flowers.

HANGING ARRANGEMENTS FROM WALLS AND CEILINGS

CHARACTERISTICS OF HANGING ARRANGEMENTS
Among the places which can be decorated with ikebana is the open space within a room, a space which can be filled by containers suspended from the ceiling, walls or pillars.

As easy methods of arranging flowers, these methods are gaining in popularity. The 3 characteristics of hanging arrangements are as follows:

First, they take up very little room. Unlike ikebana for tables or shelves, they present little or no hindrance to movement. Hanging arrangements can be effectively used even in small rooms.

Second, they make an effective display with only a few plants. Even in a large room or against a large wall, an understated arrangement can be more eye-catching than a grandiose floral display.

Third, as is true for *moribana* and *nage-ire*, containers intended for a variety of purposes can be used.

Height, Place and Materials

The height at which to display hanging ikebana is a key point. Ikebana suspended from the ceiling is usually fixed so that the bottom of the container is at the eye level of a standing person. Ikebana hanging from a wall is usually kept so that the top of the container is at eye level.

However, these are not ironclad rules. The height may be adjusted according to the conditions of the room, the nature of the material or the intention of the arranger.

Arrangements suspended from above may be hung from a hook or eye driven into the ceiling. Or, a diagonal crosspiece may be attached to the walls in a corner, and an arrangement may be suspended from it by a chain or cord.

For wall arrangements, a hook or L-shaped nail may be driven into the wall. In both cases, the containers must be suspended by a cord, wire or chain.

Using plant material that grows in cascading forms is especially effective for these arrangements.

Making a Suspended Arrangement

Let us practice with an easy-to-make arrangement. The container is an ordinary basket and the plant materials are mountain lilies and golden cockscomb.

1. Attach 3 lengths of cord to the basket.
2. Place a small, low vessel in the middle of the basket; an empty can may be used.
3. Determine the place to be decorated and hang the basket. Put a frog in the can and add water to the top of the pins. Use a lily for the arrangement's long stem and see how it looks in the basket, checking direction and angle.

4. Having decided what to do, insert the lily in the frog. Use your free hand to support the basket from the bottom.

5. Take the basket down before arranging the second flower. Always work over a a table after the first stem is arranged. Place the second lily in the center, leaning forward. This is the medium stem.

6. Place the third lily, as the short stem, to the front. This completes the framework of the finished arrangement.

7. Let us look at the front. The upright pattern formed by the 3 branches is evident.

8. Hang the basket and check the arrange-

ment's appearance. Think about the best way to add the 'assistant.'

9. Add the cockscomb, as the 'assistant,' from the rear of the basket. Now, also, support the basket with your free hand. This should be done whenever arranging material while the container is hanging.

10. Add 3 more cockscomb flowers, cut shorter than the medium stem, between the lilies. Remove unnecessary or damaged leaves.

Hanging a Container from a Wall

There are no special ways to arrange flowers preparatory to hanging them from a wall or ceiling different from *moribana* and *nage-ire* techniques. Although it appears bothersome to have to hang the container, when one gets to arranging, it is found to be not so troublesome at all. The only extra work involves attaching a cord or wire, which takes only a few moments, so by all means add this variety of ikebana to your repertoire.

For wall arrangements, a wire may be wound around the neck of narrow-necked bottles, such as deluxe liquor bottles or decanters, and a loop made in the back. The bottle then can be suspended from the loop. Always make certain that the wire or cord is strong enough to support the container with water and, if used, a frog.

Let us practice making a hanging arrangement using a basket.

1. Pass a length of cord through the base of a handle.
2. Tie it loosely.
3. Make a loop.
4. Cut any superfluous cord.

1

2

3

4

5. Place a container or can to hold water in the basket.

6. Hang the basket by slipping the loop over a nail or hook in the wall or pillar.

7. Arrange the flowers (here, cosmos) freely in the container, keeping in mind the creation of a good contrast with the rough texture of the basket. A cross support has been used for this *nage-ire* arrangement, and a lily added as an 'assistant.'

5

6

EXAMPLES OF WALL AND CEILING ARRANGEMENTS

As mentioned previously, wall and ceiling arrangements can be effective with a minimum of materials, but when places such as a salon are to be decorated, ceiling arrangements often must be large. Wall arrangements in such places, however, do not need a heavy support. In general, wall arrangements can be considered appropriate to small rooms.

Following are some examples of wall and ceiling arrangements.

7

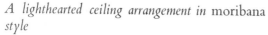

A lighthearted ceiling arrangement in moribana *style*

This is a spreading *moribana* arrangement of camellia, pine and lily in a light basket woven of bamboo. A low can for water and the frog have been placed in the basket. A fresh feeling is imparted by the red camellia, fresh green pine needles and white lily.

A showy nage-ire *arrangement*

A sunflower in the center and ample evening mist to the left and right have been matched to this glass vase. A modern contrast has been achieved by the powerful clarity of the sunflower and the soft delicacy of the evening mist. A gladiolus extended well out to the left adds an accent. Jumbled wire and a moon-shaped frog are used to hold the material.

A fairly large arrangement, this will especially complement a dignified room or a salon.

Decorating a wall with a moribana *arrangement*

Here is a classic-looking arrangement, effec-

tive against a broad expanse of wall but using little material. Marguerites stand out in radiant spots in the front, and the lily is placed low in the container. The hemp palm leaves are arranged so that just one lightly curves downward. This fresh ikebana can be easily made by anyone. Add a little variety by letting one marguerite lean away from the rest.

Mountain ash and lily in a nage-ire *arrangement* A cord loop was made and attached to the rear of the basket. An empty juice can, which is not visible, was used for water, and a cross support was inserted into its top. The texture of the mountain ash and the lines of the branches harmonize quite well with the rattan basket.

CHAPTER 7

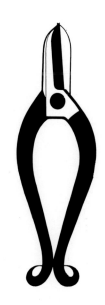

Arranging Fruits and Vegetables

Since the purpose of ikebana is basically the appreciation of plants, it is proper that fruits and vegetables be included. Before cooking and eating them, fruits and vegetables may be arranged for appreciation. Especially appropriate for the kitchen table, such arrangements bring the bounty of nature before our eyes.

The rules for arranging fruits and vegetables basically are the same as for flowers.

ANYTHING CAN BE ARRANGED IN ANYTHING

Seeing the Beauty of Materials

Learning the techniques of arranging flowers is, of course, essential if ikebana is to be mastered, but the training of a discerning eye is by no means less important.

The beauty of flowers, which seemed vague before, becomes, through the process of practicing ikebana, something very real and familiar. One realizes, for instance, that carnations and roses have stems which arch in graceful parabolas crowned by glowing flowers, and that this is where they get their liveliness.

One discovers new beauty where it previously was not seen, and one becomes able to discern how flowers will appear more beautiful when looked at from a certain direction.

Simultaneous with becoming able to distinguish between the different types of beauty, in time you will become aware of the beauty of harmonies, such as pine combined with rose, or a bough of autumn leaves and several chrysanthemums. Although materials look beautiful individually, in combination a different kind of beauty is developed.

To arrange flowers successfully, one must have a discriminating eye toward plants and be able to apply this discrimination to the techniques used.

The Trick to Combining Materials

When 2 kinds of materials are combined, both exhibit a beauty which was not revealed separately. Arranging materials in combination in ikebana is a simple matter; the standards for making combinations are as follows.

1. Mixing branches and herbaceous material: Examples of impressive combina-

A good example of a *moribana* arrangement combining the green of pine, white camellias and the red fruit of smilax.

tions are pine and rose, pussy willow and tulip, mountain ash and lily, and a bough of autumn leaves and chrysanthemums.

2. Foliage for graceful flowers: A good harmony can be produced by combining the leaves and foliage of asparag s, cycads, fatsia, ferns and the like with graceful flowers such as roses, carnations, tulips, lilies, and gerbera, or large, bold flowers such as peonies, hydrangeas, dahlias and chrysanthemums.

3. Mix several varieties of small flowers. When arranging plants which bear small flowers, use 2 or 3 varieties.

The above represent the essential standards for combining materials. In addition, among the flowers which are effective in creating a special feeling when used alone are camellias, narcissus, cherry, peonies, iris, clematis, cosmos, and roses.

An arrangement with fruit and a vegetable. Materials: carnation, apples, turnip.

Mushrooms and pine needles added to this *moribana* combination of smilax and chrysanthemums in a basket impart the feeling of autumn. Fruits and nuts are often used this way in ikebana.

Even the horsetail, the buds of which appear in spring, can be arranged with flowers. Here, it is arranged in a water pitcher with camellia foliage. A camellia flower was placed nearby.

148

Two pieces of driftwood have been joined and a single hydrangea flower used for this ikebana. An empty can was attached to the rear of the driftwood and the flower placed in it.

GETTING HINTS FROM COLOR AND FORM

How can one get hints for making combinations? First of all, look at the flowers' colors, and combine complementary colors or contrast opposing colors with the same sense that you use in selecting and combining articles of clothing.

Concerning form, the flowers—and leaves —can be said to have as much variety as people's faces, and there may be great variation within the same species. You have to pick out those which form harmonious combinations.

UTILIZE ALL FORMS OF PLANTS

Ikebana is the art of using all forms of plants.

Buds and flowers, new foliage and autumnal foliage, stems and branches—all are used in ikebana. It is characteristic of ikebana that— in addition to the ordinary plants and flowering trees—shrubs, foliage plants, water plants, autumn leaves, berries, vines, and even roots, and also seaweed, vegetables, fruit, tree roots and driftwood are all used. Because we say 'flower arranging' does not mean we have to limit ourselves to flowers.

ARRANGEMENTS CAN BE MADE IN ANYTHING

As has been indicated, many types of containers can be used for ikebana—bowls, jars, vases, basins, compotes and the like—and whether *nage-ire* or *moribana* arrangements

149

arrangement. This shows one way even an extremely narrow-mouthed container can be used. The nature of the materials has been utilized in a very light, casual arrangement.

A strong flower for a wine bottle

Although also a narrow-mouthed container, this wine bottle is not suited for weak-looking flowers. Two sunflowers, together with some wisteria vine which provides a bold and irregular line, have been used, resulting in an ikebana brimming with vitality. Pick a liquor bottle with a design potential that appeals to you, and arrange matching flowers in it.

are to be made is determined by the container. Just as anything can be arranged, arrangements can be made in any kind of container, whether it be a household utensil or anything else. Some unusual containers are shown here as examples of what can be done.

Open a window in a bundle of straw

A container has been wrapped in straw (in Japan, saké bottles are sometimes protected this way) and an opening cut in the straw to permit the materials, camellia and smilax berries, to be inserted. This is a cascading *nage-ire* arrangement. The restrained color of the straw harmonizes well with the warmth of the plant materials.

A delicate arrangement

Clematis and variegated pampas grass have been used in this natural-looking *nage-ire*

JAPANESE FESTIVAL IKEBANA

Flowers for New Year's Day

New Year is by far Japan's most popular holiday, and it is also the most serious holiday of all. The celebration of the coming of the New Year is accompanied by expressions of hope for luck in the coming year and by an exchange of social visits. The holiday is observed on a national scale, much as Christmas is in Western countries.

Standard materials for ikebana made for the New Year include pine, which is evergreen and grows upright in a stately and dignified way, bamboo, which bends without breaking, and flowering plum, which blooms despite cold temperatures. Peony is another flower favored for New Year's ikebana, and here it is combined with pine, in a classic arrangement.

This type of arrangement is found in *tokonoma* alcoves throughout the country, together with decorations such as the one here, featuring white ricecakes and other felicitious symbols.

FLOWERS FOR GIRL'S DAY

March 3 is Girl's Day, when families throughout the country display their collections of dolls, many of which may have been handed down in the family for generations. It is a day of celebration which is a major event for all Japanese girls.

In addition to the display of dolls, which are placed on a red cloth covering a tiered dais, the ikebana made for the occasion usually includes branches of the flowering peach, which blooms just at this time of year. Here, snow willow has been paired with roses. In recent years, roses and tulips have become popular replacements for peach boughs.

Flowers for Children's Day

May 5 is Children's Day, and is celebrated especially by boys and their families, in contrast to March 3, which is the corresponding holiday for girls. Both holidays have a long history in Japan and there are many customs associated with them. On Children's Day, for example, many homes are decorated with a samurai's helmet (an actual one which is a family heirloom or else a model), and paper or cloth carp are flown from tall poles set up outside. The carp is considered a particularly valiant fish, and a long-lived one as well.

On this day it is also customary to use irises in flower arrangements; the straight lines and colors of the flowers are considered befittingly masculine. Here, irises have been arranged in an upright ikebana in combination with a samurai doll.

FLOWERS FOR MOON VIEWING

Moon viewing is a typically Japanese activity. This arrangement, made at the time of the full harvest moon in September, includes pampas grass plumes, a head of millet, chrysanthemums, Chinese bellflowers and asters. The arrangement has been combined with rice-cakes, the traditional offerings to the moon. This arrangement is meant to be appreciated at the time when the moon is most beautiful, during the clear September weather.

The calligraphy on the scroll is the ideograph for moon.

定価3,000円
in Japan